Campfire Conversations

by Will Moody

wbmoody@netspace.net.au

ISBN No 978-1-291-10673-2

available online from
www.Lulu.com

Introduction

Having over the past few years written, re-written, polished, demolished and, finally, abolished reams of putative "poetry" to the re-cycle bin, I find there is still a resistant remnant that I realise I am reluctant to relinquish (see footnote). But, what to do with this refractory remnant? Fortunately (for me anyway), the era of "any dill can get their drivel published" is upon us. There are any number of websites through which the non-gender-specific dill can download his or, as it may be, her "masterpiece" and, with minimal effort and at reasonable cost, become a "published author" almost overnight!

So, being at least as big a dill as most other dills, I now join the exponentially multiplying ranks of "published authors" with this volume which contains, I think, a fairly representative selection of my particular brand of drivel.

Mind you, judgeing by what is offered by way of entertainment in our magazines and on our radios and T.V. sets these days, drivel seems to be very popular right now. So who knows? Perhaps...if you prefer your drivel served up in the form of rhyming verse...some portions of this book might be to your taste.

Stranger things have happened.

Acknowlegements

To all those who have humoured me...um...I mean, encouraged me and generously offered me the benefit of their knowlege and experience, I am most grateful. Notable among these are Jim Haynes, Carol Heuchan, Jim Brown and members of the Australian Bush Poets Association website forum. I hope that one or two of these rhymes may justify your optimism.

Lastly, it is surely only the wife or husband of a person suspected of having "poetic tendencies" who can appreciate the peculiarities of day to day life with such a creature. That my wife Mary was able to adjust to the discovery that I was such a person after 43 years is a tribute to her adaptability. Thanks Luv.

Will Moody

(Footnote: for the uninitiated, the foregoing is an example of "all-litter-ation" because it is often found littering the works of amateur poets. I do what I can to preserve traditions)

Contents

Section 1

Rural Views

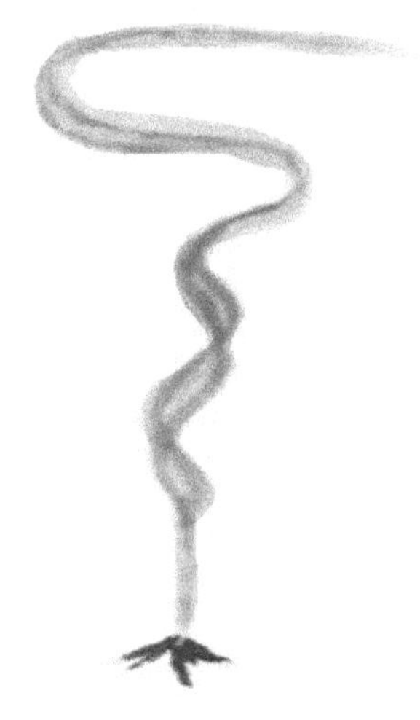

Moonrise

Beneath an awesome canopy of star encrusted sky,
scintillating sparks rise from my camp-fire, floating high.
There's muted conversation, as I nurse a mug of tea,
with Ned who sprawls with head on paws...his eyes, half closed, on me.

A line of hills are shadows, merely deeper than the rest.
There's silence all around me, now each bird has gone to nest.
Then liquid luminescence 'cross the quiet landscape spills,
as the moon climbs slowly skyward from behind the brooding hills.

With an eerie sense of stillness, stretching to infinity,
she paints the scene with pearl dust, silhouetting rock and tree.
In the soft and silken silence, into peaceful sleep I fall,
as a mopoke greets the moonrise with a distant ghostly call.

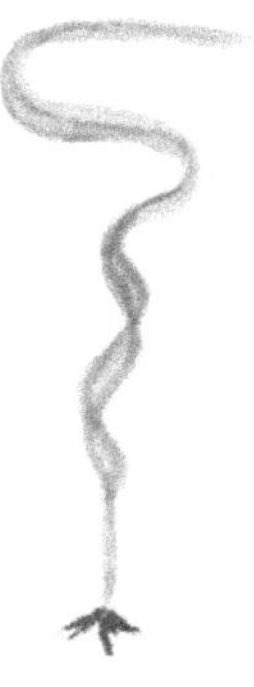

A Campfire Gathering

It seems that if you live in town,
you're sure to have some bumptious clown
from council round to shut you down
    if you should light a campfire.
And yet, the thought occurs to me...
where would this wide brown country be
without a pot of hot, strong tea
    brewed on a blazing campfire?

How far would pioneers have got
in some remote and lonely spot?
Could they have made it? I think not
    ...without a homely campfire.
At end of day with coming night,
a swaggy's mood turned to delight,
his spirits soaring at the sight
    of smoke trails from a campfire.

Our heroes out of yesteryear...
what was the thing *they* held most dear
(next to their dog and horse and beer) ?
    ...a bright and cheery campfire!
They'd reminisce and they'd recall
gun-shearers; teamsters; drovers tall
...and roads they'd travelled most of all...
    while hunkered round a campfire.

The comradeship that they found there
with songs and yarns and jokes to share
...they'd say there's nothing to compare
    with old mates round a campfire!
Uncounted campfires light our past.
They're dotted right across this vast
and varied land...but fading fast...
    those pale and ghostly campfires.

For now it seems, at least in town,
that you're an inconsiderate clown
(*and* an adjectival noun)
          to light a flamin' campfire.
Can *we* let this tradition die?
Sit idly by and heave a sigh
for 'olden days' when you and I
          once shared a friendly campfire?

It's not like this world can afford
to leave abandoned and ignored
the fellowship and *bon accord*
          that's found around a campfire!
I hope there's still some left who know
the magic of a campfire's glow
...outside the towns...and who still go
          and gather, round a campfire.

Perhaps the gidgee still burns bright ...
its sparks ascending...points of light
against the vast, black dome of night
          that crowds around their campfire.
Perhaps some night I'll find them there
and, as those sparks rise like a prayer,
I'll say "G'day...mind if I share
          this night around your campfire?"

A Country Wife

I'm sure you must have seen her as you've walked along the street,
unless you never stray from city life.
But if you visit country towns, you're almost sure to meet
a woman you might call..."a country wife'.

She might be wearing work boots with some faded old blue jeans ;
a shirt to make her city cousins smirk.
A look that won't be found in glossy fashion magazines
and, like as not, it's her own handiwork.
She might live raising sheep or wheat or on a dairy farm;
be blonde, brunette or something in between.
Her brown or blue or green eyes have a sort of naïve charm,
her arms and face glow with a golden sheen.

Her features might seem unrefined when taken at first glance,
the imprint of her life is there to trace.
But if a smile lights up her face, when given half a chance,
a sudden transformation will take place.
She goes about her business with a sure and steady gait
and idleness is something she can't stand.
The firmness of her handshake is enough to demonstrate
the legacy of life spent on the land.

Her gentle strength and friendliness and confidence implies
ability to make the best of things;
to take charge in a crisis should emergencies arise
and face the challenge every new day brings.
It might be helping with a fence or bringing in a crop,
or pulling up some vegies gone to seed.
Or fetching fertilizer from the local produce shop,
or spraying herbicide on brush and weed.

These same hands are the ones that knit and crochet for a friend
some baby clothes or other fancy things.
Or when her own child's in a play, she knows she can depend
on Mum to whip her up some angel's wings.
Her arts and crafts are legend in the townships round about,
she quilts and paints and potters with the best.
Her wholesome country cooking is a treat without a doubt,
as any famished farmhand will attest.

She's hostage to the weather, as most country people are,
it's not just something on the evening news,
and bushfire, flood and drought she's had to battle through so far...
she doesn't have the luxury to choose.
Locust plagues and cattle ticks are things *you* can ignore;
for people on the land, they're *very* real.
Her family must face up to these things and so much more
before *yours* can enjoy their evening meal.

And when somebody needs a little tender loving care,
these same hands show surprising gentleness.
When someone is in trouble she has always time to spare.
It wouldn't cross her mind she could do less.
She's active in her Rotary, the local P & C
and member of the local Landcare crew.
She volunteers with Red Cross and supports Camp Quality.
Yes, she's a 'Country Woman' through and through.

So stop and give a second thought if there should chance to be
a woman like her walking down your street.
We couldn't get along without these country wives, you see...
They help to keep this nation on its feet.

Clearance Sale

"Now here's a bit of top-notch stuff,
let' s see - lot one three four.
I've seen these go two thousand each
down at the agent's store.

Who'll start me with two hundred?
Only ten per cent at that.
Come on, who'll get me started?
There's One hundred! Thank you Pat."

There's lots of locals in the yard, but bidding's pretty slow.
There's not much cash to spare round here, and mate, I ought to know.
"One twenty at the front now!
There's one thirty at the back!
No advance?..Last call!..Last chance!
One forty! ..Thank you Jack."

Young Clarrie Spence, the auctioneer, he's working flamin' hard
to try and get the most for Jim before he clears the yard.
And Jack's got troubles of his own. He can't afford that gear.
He'll use up all his overdraft, things don't pick up this year.

I know just how he's feeling though. We've had these sales before.
The way this drought is dragging on, we'll likely see lots more.
And Clarrie...he's a job to do...*and* five mouths to feed.
It's not his fault that Jim's sold up to meet shareholders' greed.

It's not the first old neighbour's farm they've seen in recent years
that's gone under the hammer and they're not the first wife's tears
to be held back while strangers pack the only home she's known.
He's not the first good mate they've seen and thought "How old he's grown."

This farm's been worked by Thomsons for a hundred years or more.
Jim's grand-dad used to be the mayor, before the first World War.
His father was a Digger too; we all remember Joe.
He must be turning in his grave to see the old place go.

Who me? I run the local bank...the villain of the piece.
Yes, I was born and bred round here. I married Jimmy's niece.
So don't think I don't feel their pain and lose my share of sleep.
It isn't me has much to gain when some-one's in too deep.

I've got a mortgage of my own... and fifty four years old.
When Head Office makes decisions I must do what I am told.
But, mine's the only face they see when they think of the bank...
and in their minds it seems to be it's me they have to thank.

Ah well, I've got my job to do...like Clarrie, he's got his.
We neither one might like it, but that's just the way it is.

"I thank you for your patience gents.
Next up, lot one four o.
Instructions are to clear the lot
and everything must go."

Song Lines

The Song Lines of our Country
are all fading, one by one.
The Songs that bound our ancient land,
since Dreaming was begun.
Ten thousand elders, gone before,
the sacred Songs held dear,
and chanted them uncounted times
for all the tribes to hear.

The Songs Lines told the stories
of shifting desert sand;
of caves in the high country
where snow topped mountains stand.
Of gibber plains and wetlands,
the home of jabiru;
of hidden springs and oyster coves;
Ooldea and Kakadu.

So that this land's own people
when they wandered far and wide,
could find the soaks and water holes
and creeks to camp beside.
So they could find the right track
to other tribes' country,
when all would come together
to hold corroboree;

to trade and learn the legends;
to hunt and make new ties;
to dance the sacred dances
beneath the full moonrise.
By years of occupation
old ways were forced to change.
By settlers, towns and fences
country changed to something strange.

Our tribal laws were weakened.
White Fella's law was strong.
From sacred sites and waterholes
they made us " move along ".
So many elders slaughtered,
so many wounds and wrongs...
so many children taken
before they heard the songs.

The Song Lines are all fading...
but Country's singing yet.
For this our land is ancient,
and Country don't forget.
It's not too late to listen.
Don't have to live apart.
For Country is still singing,
if you listen with your heart.

Meeting Place

Come with us on a journey,
suspend your disbelief.
Come and share our Dreamtime,
and give your soul relief.

Come meet our Rainbow Serpent,
who carved the riverbed.
Sit at Japara's campfire
with Yiwarra overhead.

Come and share the Dreaming,
and at the end of night,
let Goo-goor-gara wake you
at cold dawn's fire light.

Listen to our legends.
See our ancient art.
Look with eyes wide open,
and listen with your heart.

Talk *with* me, not *at* me,
We can be reconciled.
Who-ever our Creator,
we all are some-one's child.

Japara..................the Moon Man of Dreamtime legends. The moon is his campfire.
Yiwarra ....the Milky Way in Dreamtime legends.
Goo-goor-gara... the Kookaburra.

Essences

In churches with steeples, in penance and prayer...
in psalter and scripture, some seek their God there.
My God's not confined to a building or book...
I walk in his presence wherever I look.

The moon when it's rising; the sun as it sets.
The stars that grow brighter the darker it gets.
The canyons of cloud thrusting into the sky;
the flashes of lightning that dazzle the eye.

The crumpled, old mountains with snow in their hair;
the fields of wildflowers their lower slopes bear.
The bend of a river...the arc of a beach,
the towering tree-tops...the flesh of a peach.

The flight of a feather; the faith of a dog.
The lichen and moss on a rainforest log.
The smell of the earth with the coming of rain.
The breezes that riffle the pages of grain.

A high-country track and a wilderness path.
The songs of the birds in the storm's aftermath.
The whales as they gambol at play in the bight.
The silence that settles on deserts at night.

The sweep of the plains reaching out without end
like wide-flung brown arms of a welcoming friend.
The land's changing seasons; the tide's ebb and flow.
The blue sky above me. The red earth below.

The wonder of child-birth...the mysteries of death.
The tentative step and the faltering breath.
The cycles of nature; the spirit of place...
these are the altars where I find God's grace.

“Have-a-Chat”

They used to call him “Have-a-Chat” in true laconic style,
for when he spoke his words were sparse and spare.
As oft as not delivered with a sort of bashful smile,
and usually, a melancholy air.
His clothes had seen far better days, his hair was thin and grey;
his shoulders slumped; with age his back was bent.
But though he might have seemed a relic from a bygone day,
his bearing let you know he was a gent.

At pension time or thereabouts, he’d come in from the scrub
to fill his scripts and buy a bit of grog.
And then he’d get a counter lunch down at the local pub
and share it with his old blue heeler dog.
They say he had a humpy way out back of Larsen’s place,
and rumour spoke about a long dead wife.
But no-one ever bothered him, accepted with good grace
as just another face of country life.

Around about this time last year, the old bloke failed to show.
He wasn’t missed ’til three days overdue.
Clarrie at the cop shop said “ I s’pose I’d better go
and see what’s up”. I said that I’d come too.
Old Clarrie had a fair idea where Have-a-Chat might be.
It seems he once had stumbled on a camp.
He was well respected in our bush community
and in the scrub, Old Clarrie was a champ.

He soon tracked down the humpy in some trees beside a creek
and quietly, we went and looked inside.
We reckoned that the poor old bloke was dead less than a week,
but he wasn’t on his lonesome when he died.
He looked like he was sleeping, on his rough old camping bed
and, somehow, he looked younger and at rest.
The old dog never shifted, and we knew he too was dead.
It lay there with its head upon his chest.

.....oooOooo.....

That Saturday a few of us had gathered at the pub
to have a few to toast old Have-a-Chat.
The conversation centred on the old man's funny ways
and how each one remembered this and that.
They wondered where he'd lived and what he'd done before he came;
did he ever have a wife and kids in tow ?
I said "William never married. That was Have-a-Chat's real name.
My uncle, if you really want to know."

"My mother's older brother, William Reilly...Uncle Bill.
Saw action at Kokoda, World War Two.
Got caught right in the thick of it...the fight at Buna Hill.
Came out alive and got a medal too.
He lost a lot of mates up there, and saved more than a few.
A lot of brave Australian blood was spilt.
He came back home a hero for the things he had to do,
but somehow, burdened with a sense of guilt."

"That he was still alive, but in his mind there were engraved
the names of mates he'd left there on the track.
It didn't seem to help much, thanks to him some men were saved.
Like my dad Steven Larsen, made it back."
So in the final wash-up I don't know which one went first;
which one was first to knock on heaven's gate.
But in my own opinion, Have-a-Chat's heart fairly burst...
he just couldn't bear to leave another mate.

High-Country Hike

Kosciusko has a mantle of snow,
now that winter is flexing its grip.
As the fresh breeze abates, laboured breathing creates
a frosting of ice on my lip.

Under brilliant blue skies, with familiar surprise,
I drink in the High-Country show.
A short moment to rest, one quick glance to the crest,
and onward and upwards I go.

In the cold crystal light, all the colours are bright
on the trunks of the snow-gum tableau,
as they writhe to a song, slow and ancient but strong,
only sap, soil and sinew can know.

I am feeling my age as I reach the last stage
and my shoulders are starting to sag.
Every step seems to make every leg muscle ache
with my spirits beginning to flag.

But it seems now I hear, with the summit so near,
phantom words of a whispered refrain
that keep urging me on 'til my tiredness is gone,
and I bend to my task once again.

Now at last at the top, gear and backpack I drop
and my lungs seem to tear with each gasp.
Standing hands upon knees, aches and pains slowly ease,
and success is secure in my grasp.

All the hubbub that drowns us in cities and towns;
all the fear and the doubts melt away.
My horizons expand to encompass the land...
and I'm top of the world...for today.

A Drifter's Dream

I lie beside my campfire in the night
and gaze up at the stars I'm lying under...
and wonder if this wanderlust will last
until I've seen the last horizon's wonder.

Will age and circumstances co-conspire
to bring my earthly travels to an end,
while still unsatisfied my heart's desire
to see what lies beyond the river's bend ?

Or slog among the sand-dunes in the deserts
that span the scene beyond the blackened stump.
To range along the rocky gorges' courses,
where swollen rivers surge and suck and pump.

God grant that, when He takes me to His presence
to judge my thoughts and deeds for good or ill,
He sentences my soul to roam Australia,
'til of this wide brown land I've had my fill.

To wander, with the changeing of the seasons,
from balmy coast to frosty mountain air.
From gibber plain to misty forest gully.
God, grant that I might spend forever there.

Breath of Life

Son of Soil,
Salt of Earth,
years of toil
yours by birth.
Daily prayer…
faith devout.
Breathing in…
breathing out.

Take a wife…
heart of gold.
Welcome more
to the fold.
Sturdy sons…
how they sprout!
Breathing in…
breathing out.

Now the years
that were blessed
give way to
times that test.
Facing floods…
battling drought.
Breathing in…
breathing out.

Your best years
slipping by.
Debts mount up…
cares pile high.
Rising fear…
constant doubt.
Breathing in…
breathing out.

Little left
of your dream.
Broken heart's
silent scream.
Giving in.
Clearing out.
Breathing in…
breathing out.

Wife and kids,
farm too, gone.
What use now
to go on?
Life and Death
turn about...
breathing in…..

Song and Silence

(Her Beauty and Her Terror)

Song...

Deep and black, Night's drapes are drawing slowly back from Dawn's faint light ...
Sun, above horizon clawing, surges forward into sight.
Soon, his flame the bush enlightens to the news of Day's rebirth...
as each chill, dark corner brightens, warmth and colour fill the Earth.

Kookaburra's raucous fanfare spreads the news that Night has fled,
echos ringing in the clear air, rousing neighbours from their bed.
Cockatoos, in tree-tops flocking, pass it on with squawk and screech,
all the 'sleeper-in-ers' mocking in their loud discordant speech.

Willy Wagtails start chiaking...Golden Whistlers pipe their songs.
Whipbirds practise their whip-cracking to the calls of Currawongs.
Lorikeets in noisy gaggles, discontent with status quo,
start again their constant haggles as the light begins to grow.

Wheeling skyward, mighty Wedgetail takes a condescending view
of the flighty, flitting Fantails taking flap-baths in the dew.
Glossy Blacks, the scene departing, scull sedately through the air
while the Martins - diving, darting - show them how it's done with flair.

Dew-drenched, guarded gullies thrilling as the Shrike-thrush grey and shy,
with his liquid, fluted trilling, flings *bel cantos* to the sky.
Bellbirds with exquisite timing, hidden somewhere safe from view,
add sweet accents with their chiming...peeping ducklings form a queue.

Magpies lift their heads and carol...all the bushland choir rejoice.
Each his own distinct apparel...each his own distinctive voice.
Is there anyone who's witnessed such a morning, such a scene
and, conceding He existed, not thought : "Here, God's hand has been" ?

And Silence...

Yet, the same hand that created such a peaceful scene as this,
smites the land with drought-breath baited with a fatal searing kiss.
Wasted, withered grasslands dying, watercourses parched and dry...
breathless birds, too weak for flying, fall bewildered from the sky.

Sheep and cattle and wild horses, parchment skins and death's-head grins,
stagger through the arid courses where hope fails and death begins.
Where the drying wind's long threnody keens wierdly on the air...
when the country sings no song except the silence of despair.

Heath and forest ranges burning...man and beast in fear and pain...
man and beast and country yearning for the healing touch of rain...
Is there no-one who's not cried on such a God-forsaken day
"If there is a God in Heaven ...why then has He turned away ?"

Cold Camp-fires

Cold, black embers of old camp-fires that have long since lost their glow...
in their shadows I see faces of old mates I used to know.
Friendly, old familiar faces, down the years gone separate ways,
from their dark and distant places come in shades of ghostly greys.

All those mates, long-since departed, they come to the curlew's call
and they join me round the campfire as the evening shadows fall.
And we share the easy mateship of the fire-light's ebb and flow,
as we did when we were drovers on the Barkly...years ago.

With the fitful sparks ascending high into the chill night air,
hands and rumps by turn are toasting in the gidgee's rosy glare.
Then the brew is pouring, steaming, into battered mugs of tin,
with perhaps some extra flavour from a splash of rum or gin.

As the full moon clears the ridge-line shedding pale and powdered light,
now and then the hobbled horses whinny to us in the night.
And the cattle, softly lowing all around us on the plain,
mill and shuffle round a moment and then settle down again.

Thin, faint echoes of bush ballads blend beneath a star-strewn sky
with the murmur of the she-oaks as a night breeze wanders by...
raucous shouts and scornful laughter greet the end of some tall tale...
...ah, but they're only fading fragments of long nights shared on the trail.

--->>0<<---

Yes, they're only recollections, but a comfort nonetheless,
for they keep an old man comp'ny...help to fill the emptiness.
Still, I know that soon I'll meet again those phantoms from the past,
and we'll share another camp-fire...when my journey's done at last.

Then we'll stir those embers up again and pass the pouch around...
yarns about old times and places we'll be sharing, I'll be bound.
And we'll sing again the old songs while we watch the billy brew,
and old friendships we'll rekindle...soon...
when I'm cold ashes too.

Section 2

Past Masters

A Song That Lingers On

Some knew him just as "Harry" or, when fancy took, "Joe Swallow."
He told the tales of New South Wales; of tracks he used to follow.
And in his rhymes we glimpse the times of sunburnt plains and men...
of drovers' ways and gold-rush days. The world was wide back then.

A good part of his life was spent in wearing out his shoes
on dusty plains and cobbled lanes, while following his muse.
How often did the lines she hid resolve within his head
along some track, somewhere outback, while tramping to a shed?

The ragged bums in city slums weren't strangers to his eyes.
He'd seen his share of mis'ry there and he could sympathise.
His poet's eye was smitten by the "faces in the street"
as much as by the outback sky and dust and blinding heat.

From run-down boarding houses to a played out digger's drive,
the places and the faces in his writings come alive.
And by his pen there lives again a time that's now long gone.
His legacy, to you and me ...a song that lingers on.

C J Dennis Style

"In the style of C J Dennis...";
what a mountain peak to climb!
And where on earth's a bloke supposed to start ?
Should he 'ave a go like Ginger Mick
at makin' slangwidge rhyme
while tearin' proper English words apart ?

Or write another Austra-Laise
fer blokes an' coves an' coots
ter sing as they go marchin' orf ter war ?
But then, a bloke like Digger Smith...
he wouldn't give two hoots.
He'd want to know what all the fuss was for.

Another style a bloke might try
is writing like a Glug
to satirise the games that people play.
King Splosh is still incompetent;
Sir Stodge is still a mug...
some people act like Glugs right to this day.

They still want their "pianers
and their pickles" for some stones
while industries are going to the dogs.
More plasma screens on credit cards,
more shiny mobile phones...
then wonder why they're in such debt to Ogs.

I've often thought that Den's best work
was in the style of "Wheat"...
it's a "pleasure beyond measure" just to read.
With its "sowin' things an' growin' things"...
a pulse that's hard to beat.
I'd need some help from Heaven to succeed.

Or then again, a bloke might try
to find Jim Of The Hills
in Den's much loved Toolangi On The Rise,
and write about the joy he felt
amongst the rocks and rills
to see the love reflected in Nell's eyes.

Maybe a dissertation
on the workings of the mind
of a tiny ant explorer, keen to roam ?
But travelogues are not my scene
(well, not the insect kind.)
I think I'll take a pass and stay at home.

New words that no-ones heard of
might be the way to go,
but don't know if the publishers could cope
with words that spell-check couldn't check
and dictionaries don't know...
like this..."trianti-wonti-gongalope."

Well, perhaps "The Singing Garden"
will shed light upon our path
to find the Dennis style that suits us best.
Like the sun that shone on Arden
in the winter's aftermath,
these verses might illuminate our quest ?

So, our path has many turnings
seeking "C J Dennis style"...
but all these turnings can be reconciled.
Just read again his poems
that have left you with a smile,
and re-discover your own inner child..

(composed for a competition "written in the style of C.J.Dennis")

Henry's Ghost

(for James Howard)

A cold, clear day in Gulgong for the holiday week-end,
and in the crowd that filled the streets I spotted an old friend.
I saw the ghost of Henry...he mingled in the throng
that congregated in that town close by the Cudgegong.

They'd come to share his legacy and celebrate the man
that put old Gulgong on the map, back where it all began.
They sang him "Happy Birthday", even cut a birthday cake.
In ev'ry pub, it seemed to me, they held old Henry's wake.

The whole town seemed just like a shrine, his spirit to invoke
in rhyme and song and laughter, in tribute to the bloke.
He nodded with a little smile. I proudly shook his hand.
We stood together in the street and listened to the band.

Was it really the old master, Henry Lawson that I saw?
Well, I know I'm getting old, but still, my eyesight's not that poor.
He had that yard-broom moustache, leaning slightly on his cane.
His eyes held glints of laughter, pools of wisdom...lang syne's pain.

Was he flesh or was he spirit? Me, I'm not prepared to say.
I know that there were plenty more who saw him there that day.
If his image was a spectre that must fade into the past...well...
his words still echo down the years and they, at least, will last.

ooooooooo

James Howard is a bush poetry performer often seen at bush poetry festivals and events in the persona of Henry Lawson come to life, remaining in character throughout. His presence, particularly at the annual Henry Lawson Festival in Gulgong NSW, is a feature for those who embrace the spirit of such events.

A Song of Praise

Because a prim and proper chap from Laura turned his feet
toward the tired and tawdry world of Little Lonsdale Street...
because he saw beyond the grime, the petty crime and sin
and looked into its people's hearts and saw what lay within...

Barrengarry, Bright and Broke
know the Sentimental Bloke.
Battersea and Barradine,
enchanted by his sweet Doreen.
Beerwah, Bargo, Bostobrick
grieve in turn for Ginger Mick.
Bogabilla, Bilpin, Bigga
praise the pluck of Smith the Digger.
Wollongong and Wollondilly
laugh and say that Glugs are silly.
Ipswich, Ingham, Innamincka
smile at rhymes of Sym the Tinker.
Armidale and Arayonga
ride to Cuppacumalonga.
Logan, Lawler, Leith and Laura
wander with the Ant Explorer.

On the Condamine and Barcoo...
by the Murray and the Paroo...
in the outback and the city...
on our own and in committee...
in the mine and on the station...
hearths and homes across the nation...
in the proddings of our concience,
in our national sub-conscious,
wily wit and subtle pathos
work their magic on our ethos.
In the values that we cherish
live the words that will not perish
while the wisdom that they teach us
live and down the years still reach us.

Because a very special gift was given to a man
to rhyme in such a way that neither you or I say can,
in weaving words that make us smile or, often, heave a sigh...
our lives are blessed with riches that mere money cannot buy.

Section 3

Writer's Cramp

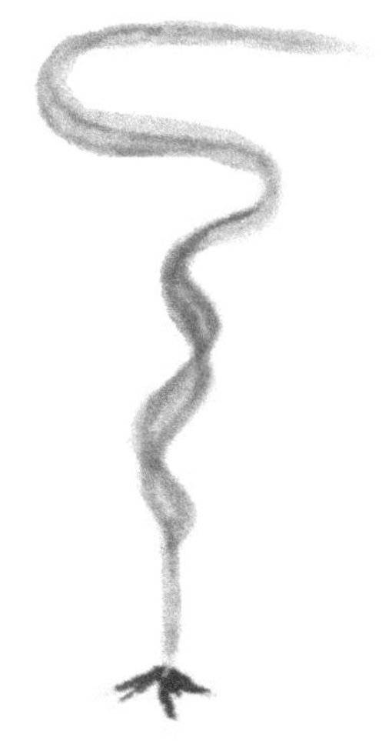

Chance or Choice

Was Henry Lawson pre-ordained to write the way he did,
or was it just a way that he could earn an extra quid ?
Was Paterson or Dennis pre-disposed to write in verse,
or merely in their time convinced a fellow could do worse ?
    Was every poet down through time,
    devoted to this paradigm,
    convinced he could live on through rhyme...
    or mindful of his purse ?

What is this strange, obsessive tilt that makes us feel compelled
to write in such a way that endings must be parallelled,
with words selected to impart a rhythm with a swing
while painting mental pictures, as the pen and wit take wing ?
    At times unbidden and unsought,
    it seems a strange affliction wrought
    upon those of a certain sort...
    A weird and wondrous thing.

And if you feel this urge in you and think you'd like to try
to make the listener laugh out loud or make the reader cry...
if in your mind words seem to string together in this way...
and feel compelled to write them down, my friend then you just may
    be one afflicted by this thing...
    You may just have a song to sing,
    and find you can't do anything...
    about it but obey.

Lost For Words

He sits there, sad and lonely, staring mutely into space;
a picture of dejection inhabiting his face.
His pen in hand, immobile; empty notebook in his lap.
My pity for him's stirring...(poor unfortunate old chap).

What can it be that ails him this witching hour of night?
What is it that impales him? What does he strive to write?
The minutes drag to hours...his pen-hand never stirs...
at times, a lowly mutter..."What rhymes with blasted 'burrs' ?"

The masters, from the bookshelves, seem to snigger and to mock.
Bereft of all ideas...tick, tock, tick, tock, tick, tock...
It's late, and I must leave him. But, hang on! Here's a shock...
This cannot be! But, yes...it's me...and I've got writer's block!

If You...

If you take me on a journey far beyond the commonplace
and tell me of the people that you've met with, face to face...
If you tell me of their triumphs; of their downfall; of their pride;
describe the way they lived their lives...and tell me how they died...
If you take me to the mountains with their ridges, crags and snow
or take me to the valleys, lying lush and green below...
If you take me to the rivers where they flow into the sea...
If you take me to the lakes that lie where old towns used to be...
If you take me where the pioneers first opened up the land
and introduce the womenfolk who stood at their right hand...
If you share with me the treasures you have laid up in your store
in your own plain, honest language...
well...I'll only ask for more.

Rhythmic Roots

We feel subconscious rhythms all around us every day.
Light comes to us each morning in the customary way
and fades again each evening as the darkness takes its course,
which lasts until the dawning...here is rhythm at its source.

We feel a different rhythm in the tidal ebb and flow.
We sense the years progressing as the seasons come and go.
And under all these rhythms, one that plays the central part...
the fundemental rhythm of the beating of your heart.

And so these rhythms move us in a real and potent sense;
the drumbeats of the present march toward the future tense.
And as these patterns move us, we seek still more rhythms out
to satisfy this craving. Is this what life's all about?

The inner man, the soul, the spirit...call it what you will...
thrives upon these rhythms and can never get its fill.
Our every breath an echo of the music of the spheres...
the rhythm of the rise and fall of our allotted years.

But, if Rhythm is the only thing we judge existance by,
our life becomes a sterile scape - tasteless - humdrum - dry.
For it's Counterpoint to rhythm that makes life worth living more...
it's Crescendo, Pause and Chord Change that adds interest to the score.

Language!

When all the living world was young, the animals and birds
communicated very well without recourse to words.
A grunt, a growl, a roar, a howl were all that were exchanged,
a hiss, a croak...then humans *spoke*...and all was re-arranged.

What were the words first uttered then? What primal sentence said?
...that phrase first heard, when meaning stirred inside another's head?
For single words might mean no more than grunt or howl or roar...
but words in combination are, potentially, much more.

It may have been a welcome or farewell or warning cry.
Was he amazed who formed the phrase that framed the first reply?
Whatever combination of the few words they then knew,
from that first primitive exchange a complex language grew.

And more than their good fortune to possess opposing thumb,
their language was the tool that paved the way for things to come.
Complex communication was an organising force
in shaping the development of mankind's future course...

shaping his society, expressing his ideas...
developing his strategies and influencing peers.
And, as his language skills evolved, he learned to write it down
inventing noun and adjective; preposition; verb; pronoun.

The 'Information Highway' that controls our world today
began with crude and simple runes incised in bits of clay.
Those simple everyday accounts of tax and harvest yields
soon led to tales of conquests won by kings on foreign fields.

And slowly down the ages, language grew from tribe to tribe,
preserved on scraps of parchment by the labour of the scribe.
Great visions of the prophets were retold throughout the land....
the news of great discoveries were passed from hand to hand.

The printing press took literacy to levels heretofore
undreamed of by the masses in the good old days of yore.
The norms that make us civilised were built up, word by word,
as Literature developed and imaginations stirred...

Now doctors practice medicine (or, if they don't, they write)
and scientists test theories out to find out if they're right..
Our jurors codify our laws to prosecute our crimes
and teachers dole out intellect...and poets meter rhymes.
Adventurers now plot a course for voyages through space...
how far can mankind's language go? ... how far the human race?

--->>0<<---

Poet?

Should he call himself a 'poet'
who can merely force a rhyme
and make words dance to cadence,
of a sort, from time to time?

Rather, call himself a 'writer'
having taken up the pen.
The offence is that much slighter
and requires less acumen.

Careful though to not claim 'author' -
'neath the sun there's nothing *new*.
Leave such labels to another.
(verdict subject to review!)

For the sole judge and sole arbiter
is good old Father Time
and the fruits are often bitter
for the harvester of rhyme.

Treasure Trove

A word unto the wise man
is sufficient, so they say.
Poets find more are required
when they join in the fray.
More words to flesh the moment
...to still the hands of time;
then sifted by the poet
to be woven into rhyme.

Words of joy and laughter;
of tales beyond belief.
Words of pure elation
and those that speak of grief.
Wasted words of warning;
words of gratitude.
Words of little value -
empty platitude.

Wild words full of fury;
words that scandalise.
Caring words and calming;
words that tantalise.
Cries of love and hatred;
words that cut and thrust.
Words to lift our spirits;
words to take on trust.

Petty words of gossip;
weighty words of worth.
Wistful words of parting;
words proclaiming birth.
Words of inspiration
and words that castigate.
Stark words of rejection;
words that come too late.

Words used as a weapon;
words that flit and flirt.
Words that come between us...
words to heal the hurt.
Words that bring together;
words that tear apart.
Words of deep reflection.
Words that touch the heart.

Words of misdirection;
faithful words and true.
Words that make no difference...
those that, somehow, do.
Words of wit and wisdom
and whispered words that woo.
Words to tell our stories...
words from me... to you.

Section 4

Furred and Feathered

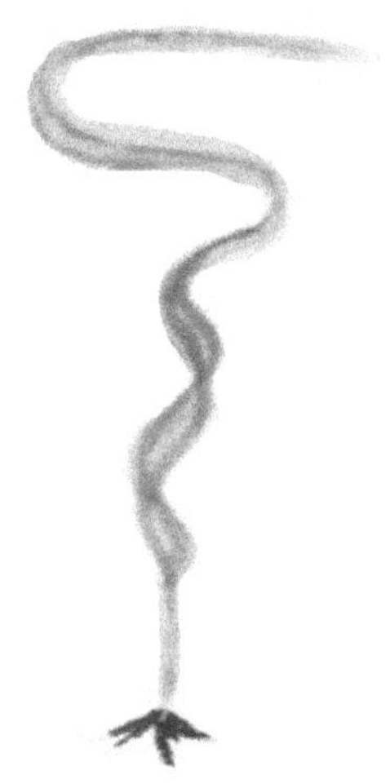

The Regent Bowerbird

It seems absurd to say a bird
you've seen gives you a thrill.
For, after all, they're just a ball
of feathers with a bill.
But when the Regent Bowerbird's observed...
I'm unreserved.

As is their way their visits may
be few and far between.
But field or park, they make their mark
wherever they are seen.
With colour splashed upon them bright and bold...
all black and gold.

But maybe "thrill" is over-kill.
There's lots of birds round here.
I don't say "Wow!" or "Holy Cow!"
whenever they appear.
But when the Regent Bowerbird's in sight...
it's sheer delight.

A Dog's Life

He took me to the beach today to swim and have a run.
Miles and miles of empty sand and boy, did I have fun!
Fetching sticks and chasing gulls, the sea and sand and sun,
I felt just like a pup again with my mate, 'Alpha One'.

I stayed close to the shallows 'coz the undertow was strong.
(I'm not a real good swimmer 'coz my legs aren't very long.)
The beach had lots of stuff to check, strange scents were all around.
I wish that he had let me keep that dead fish that I found!

I heard a noise from down below the surface of the sand.
I started digging with my paws and 'One' gave me a hand.
We never found out what it was although we moved a ton.
I nearly wagged my tail off, I was having so much fun.

I raced along the hot dry sand. I let 'er rip, full pelt,
and then jumped in the water when I felt my paws would melt.
With all that running round I soon began to feel worn out,
panting like a steam train with my tongue all hanging out.

Then my mate 'One' said "Come on boy. It's time to head for home."
We headed up the beach and left behind the sea and foam.
He said "You're looking tired, old boy. You're getting on in years".
I wagged my tail in answer and he scratched behind my ears.

And now I'm curled up in my bed with one ear cocked for him.
(I use my other senses, now my eyes are getting dim.)
He took me to the beach today...or was that just a dream?
...a happy recollection of when we made such a team.?

Kenny The Kite

Our young Square Tailed Kite is an impressive sight
when he visits and sits in our trees.
Then he scans round the house for a lizard or a mouse
just as nonchalantly as you please.

Or else takes a ride and will languidly glide
on an updraft if there is a breeze.
His eagle-eyes test for the unguarded nest
in each shrub and each tree that he sees.

All the other birds hate him and scold and berate him
for actions they view as obscene.
But it's in Nature's plan, strong ones take what they can...
it's the way that it always has been.

Killer

I had a dog called Killer, an assassin by design.
He'd murder almost daily, in weather foul or fine.
He'd hit 'em in the jugular, and shake 'em once or twice.
My word, he was a terror on all those rats and mice!

But mind, he was a city dog...he knew the street and alley.
That cattle run I took him to was unfamiliar mallee.
He thought that feral pig was just a jumped-up rat, by heck!
"I'll teach him not to come 'round here. I'll break his bloody neck!"

I miss that dog, my Killer Dog . His heart was brave and big.
The odds weren't right in that there fight...
Chihuahua versus pig !

The Mudgee Budgie

There's this bloke I knew in Mudgee,
who for years had kept a budgie,
and I tell ya, he just doted on his pet.
This chirpy little feller,
sorta green with bitsa yeller,
was his best mate from the moment that they met.

I remember one occasion,
there was 'flu about called 'Asian',
and about this time, they both began to sneeze.
Somehow, he got it in his head,
based upon some things he'd read,
that '*Bird Flu*' was the name of their disease.

And there were no guarantees
that the health authorities
wouldn't snuff his budgie if the word got out.
So he hatched a cunning plan,
"We'll go to Coonabarabran,
an' lie low with my old mate, Fritz the Kraut."

He stuffed the bird down in his trousers,
then he filled up at the bowsers,
and with grim determination, slung 'is hook.
But his plans they all unravelled
when, with barely five miles travelled,
by circumstances he was overtook.

Yes his plan, it came a cropper.
He got pulled up by a copper,
who thought..."This bloke is surely DUI."
Coz he saw that he was weaving
down the street as he was leaving,
and the copper thought he'd better find out why.

No, the copper didn't book him.
Off to hospital he took him,
coz, by now, this bloke had turned a shade of blue.
Well you shoulda seen the quacks
when they went to take his dacks,
and out of his mate's flies the budgie flew !

Now, I know that on our beaches
we see togs with funny features...
Budgie Smugglers...looking like they're gunna burst.
But Mudgee folk are not impressed,
coz they say "There's no contest."
Coz Mudgee's claim to fame?
"We had 'em first."

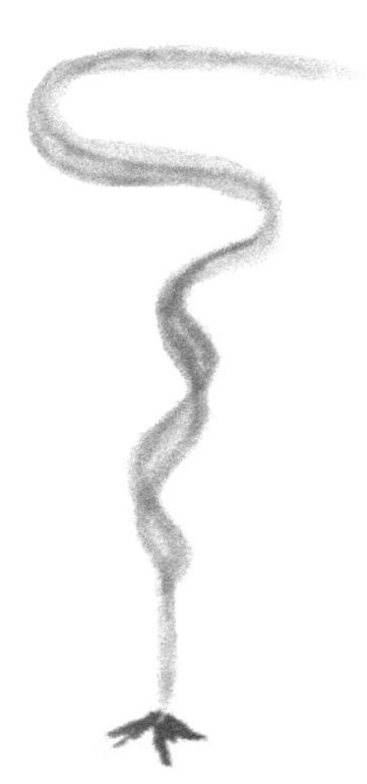

Missing Mate

I don't s'pose y've seen me dog? Been missin' these few days.
I'm gettin' sorta desp'rate...well... I'm worried anyways.
I put a notice on the board, I asked around the pub.
I looked all round the paddocks and I searched all through the scrub.

I got 'im from a friend o' mine; that was many years ago
and, strewth, weren't he a handfull, and a useless so and so.
'E wasn't much at workin' stock and never came at call.
I don't know why I kept 'im... 'ad no flamin' sense a'tall.

But then, 'e 'ad 'is moments. One night when all was dark,
'e woke me from a deep sleep with 'is wild and constant bark.
The room was full of chokin' smoke and flames licked round the door.
I wrapped a blanket round meself an' got down on the floor.

I got out through the winder, an' then when I got outside,
I started callin' for me dog... me dog what saved me hide.
'E limped around the corner, lookin' like a cast orf toy.
The flames 'ad scorched 'is ears 'an feet. I knelt 'an said..."Good boy".

I fixed 'im up as best I could. 'E's limped from that day on.
If it wasn't for that useless mutt, well mate, I'd be long gone.
When I rebuilt the humpy, I found a wooden crate
and fixed a special corner up just for me little mate.

Well, that was many moons ago...
Gawd, must be thirteen years.
Mate, keep an eye out for me dog...
you'll know 'im by 'is ears.

Tho' Love Be Blind

There's an angel at the bottom of my garden.
With wings outspread, she's fashioned out of stone.
In sun or rain she sits with features hardened
and contemplates the flowers, all alone.

Alone, that is, til someone came a'courting
last week, as Spring came laughing through the trees.
Dressed in his best tuxedo and cavorting;
advancing and retreating by degrees.

His feathers ruffed, he carolled with a passion
while she, in stoney silence, took no heed.
Convinced none could resist his Magpie fashion,
he pressed his suit, determined to succeed.

He strutted his best stuff; he posed in profile;
he fetched a juicy grub for her to taste.
He spread his wings and at her feet bowed low while
she watched emotionless, aloof and chaste.

At length the silence of his would-be lover
had his soaring ardour in retreat.
He voiced a cry, alike the lonely plover,
then flew away, crestfallen in defeat.

I wondered what it was that drew him to her...
that made him wish to share with her his nest.
Beware, lest you should meet with such a stranger...
and by her beauty be both cursed...and blessed!

The Stallion's Story

I suppose you know the story. It's a yarn that's often told
'round the campfires on a clear and starry night.
'Bout a bloke from Snowy River; but it's always left me cold:
for I've yet to hear them get the story right.

'Coz the poet bloke who wrote it left a vital detail out
of the story, though it's truthful in the main.
If you'd like to hear the whole truth (something *I* know all about),
then settle back, my friend, and I'll explain.

.....ooo0ooo.....

There was unrest in the valley, all ears pricked toward a sound
that was coming from the ridge-line to the west.
I could feel a faint vibration emanating from the ground
that made the muscles tighten in my chest.

I motioned to the brood mares they should stay just where they were
in the grassy clearing, grazing by the creek.
As I cantered at an easy pace toward the granite spur,
I saw a line of horsemen crest the peak.

I reared and screamed defiance at the riders and their mounts,
enraged that they had caught me unawares.
Then, knowing in my gut that every yard and second counts,
I wheeled and galloped back toward the mares.

All the colts and mares were milling by the big mimosa clump,
prancing nervously with panic in their eyes.
I turned and saw the riders, hell for leather from the jump,
and heard their whip-cracks and their ringing cries.

And one was flying on the wing to turn us to the right,
his stockwhip cracked like gunshots in the air.
The mares and colts stampeded in their panic and their fright;
I steered them left toward our mountain lair.

But still the riders followed, into gorges black and deep,
their stockwhips starting echoes from the walls.
And upward, ever upward, up the mountainside so steep,
I led the mob despite the risk of falls.

At last we reached the summit and the riders pulled up short
as we plunged in desperation down the side.
For the hop scrub there grew thickly. Any rider whose mount caught
on a tree root or a burrow would have died.

Then suddenly a youngster on a small and weedy beast,
gave out a yell and swung his stockwhip round.
He spurred his pony onward, never slowing in the least,
sending flint stones flying from the broken ground.

Down the hillside we went racing and then up another hill,
and still that devil drove us with his cries.
On across a grassy clearing where two mountain gullies spill,
and on to where our secret meadow lies.

But he ran us, ever onward, 'til our sides were flecked with foam;
he stuck just like a bloodhound on our track.
'Til we halted, cowed and beaten, just a few short miles from home.
He wound his stockwhip, and he turned us back.

.....ooo0ooo.....

But unseen by that horseman, one young colt had got away.
I used to know his father, old Regret.
And down by Kosciusko, where the pine-clad ridges sway,
the colt from old Regret is running yet.

But the Man From Snowy River is a household word today,
because the poet left one thing unsaid:
that the colt that they were after *beat* The Man and got away,
and leads by now a mob of fifty head.

Desert Pea

The grandson was down for a visit
and spied the old cup on the shelf.
He said to me "Pa, what's this trophy ?
Is it something that you won yourself ?"
"Got that cup for a race in The Alice.
A fine looking cup, you'll agree.
Desert Pea was the one really won it,
but they still gave the trophy to me.

I remember that race very clearly,
the weather was hot as could be.
The best mounts from all parts were gathered
and lined up against Desert Pea.
The Starter's flag dropped and we bolted.
We soon were ahead of the pack.
Just as I was counting my winnings,
a feral goat ran on the track.

Old Desert Pea shied and jumped sideways
when taken surprise by the goat.
The saddle had slipped and I uttered
some words that are not fit to quote.
The rest of the pack had rushed past us;
I knew that our chances had flown.
I desp'rately clung to the saddle
and tried to avoid being thrown.

But old D.P. he knew in a moment
that trouble was heaped on my plate.
He lifted his head and he snorted
then changed feet and altered his gait.
I regained my seat and my balance,
and to my amazement I found,
that D.P. now paced like a trotter
seeming almost to float 'cross the ground.

The gap to the leaders was closing;
the crowd was beginning to cheer.
Then with a last burst from old D.P.
we flew to the post free and clear.
My mate Desert Pea was a champion,
and tears in my eyes still well up
rememb'ring the day of our triumph;
the day we won this Camel Cup."

Wonging Faw A Wonga

I wong to see a wonga pigeon on my wawn
when at the bweak of day I stwetch and yawn.
I've seen him wots of times befaw,
but he don't come wound no maw.
Wondah wheh my Wonga Pigeon could have gawn?

That Wonga Pigeon is so sweek and vewy fat,
with bwack and white mahks on him...I wike that.
As he waddwes to and fwo,
my wuv faw him onwy gwows.
Wuv him just as much as my pet puddytat.

I am sure my pwecious puddy wikes him too,
faw I've seen him twy to say "How do you do?"
Though he cweeps up vewy quiet,
when I've seen my puddy twy it,
when my Wonga Pigeon spies him, he shoots thwough.

Wondah wheh on eawth that Wonga Pigeon is?
Shawy, someone has the answeh to my quiz?
Now I wake up evwy mawn
with a feewing so fowawn.
Wondah why he won't come wound and show his phiz?

I wouwd feed that Wonga Pigeon bwead and cawn,
and my wewcome mat wouwd neveh be withdwawn.
Oh Wonga Pigeon pwease come back,
faw my outwook's bweak and bwack.
I wong to see you, Wonga Pigeon, on my wawn.

Aquila Audax

Feel the fluid movement of the wind beneath my wings.
Rising on a thermal, I am one of Nature's kings
effortlessly gliding over valley, hill and plain.
King of Birds and ruler of a rich and rare domain...

...........I hunt again

wind-swept skies I've hunted since the days, an age ago,
this land was just emerging from the grip of ice and snow.
As lakes and seas retreated I was here to press my claim.
Long before a mountain range or river had a name...

..........the Wedgetail came.

Feather-fingered wing-tips feel for eddies in the air.
Talons, neatly folded, wait the time to stoop and tear.
Silently, I stalk across the wide Australian sky,
sudden death depending on my keen far-seeing eye...

..........I terrify

beast and bird and reptile...all are subject to my rule.
He who underestimates my talons is a fool.
Of young and old and injured, I am arbiter of fate.
Man alone disputes me, with his guns and nets and bait...

...........and manic hate.

This has been my kingdom since before the Dawn of Man.
The first who came to live here were in tune with Nature's plan.
Now, they hate and hunt me with a vengeance and a will
and hang me out on fences to proclaim their latest kill...

...........my blood they spill.

Diminished but undaunted, in these skies I yet remain.
Bloodied but unbeaten, I refuse to yield my reign.
If we lose this battle, will Man live to rue the score?
If regal wedge-tailed eagles fly Australian skies no more...

..........what lies in store?

Hear me, Aquila Audax, rightful sovereign of the air...
the serpent in his burrow and the dingo in his lair;
the glider in her tree-top and the emu on her nest...
it is *we* who are the natives, it is *we* who pass that test.

..........Which one is 'pest' ?

Section 5

Briefs

Grass Wren

Early morn.
Fluff and yawn.
Dewy grass.
Soggy arse.

Day's begun.
Golden sun
climbing high…
soon be dry.

Happy then.
Happy wren !

Rainy Day

Rainy day…
come and play.

Gutters run…
have some fun.

Twigs that float…
add leaf ...boat.

Goes so fast…
spinning past.

Dams of mud
slow the flood,

for a day,
then…wash away.

Terpsichore

How truly graceful young girls are
before they're *taught* to dance...
before they're schooled to cultivate
a boy's admiring glance.

Summertime

Weather's hot...
ocean's not.

Golden sand...
wonderland.

Break from school...
surfers rule.

Lithe of limb...
dive and swim.

Check the girls...
curves and curls.

Sea and sun...
endless fun.

Days sublime
......Summertime.

Greenhouse Effects

What a joy once in a while,
when into our car we pile,
to head off where the country air is sweet.
It puts smiles upon our faces
to discover rustic places;
the escape from urban mayhem is complete.

But, of course, in getting there
we pollute the pristine air
with "greenhouse gas" as down the road we hum.
But 'twould be an awful pity
to be stuck here in the city.
We're caught in a conundra-bloody-um !

Section 6

Pollies and Politics

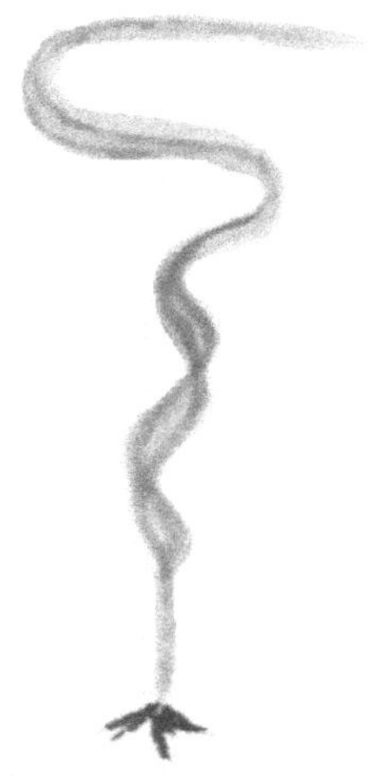

The Descent of Man: A Potted History

(with apologies to Charles Darwin)

When dinosaurs had ceased to stomp about, Neanderthal appeared and ventured out to gather food that Nature had provided where he and his new blushing bride resided. In fear and trepidation, he went forth in regions of the Hemispheric North. His world was wild, untamed and dangerous, with lions, tigers, bears…*rhinoceros.* But, thanks in part to his opposing thumb, Man prospered down the ages yet to come. To compensate for lack of fang and claw, facility with tools came to the fore.

This, coupled with a small but cunning brain, Man's dominance of Nature set in train. He set this brain to work on the construction of weapons meant for bio-mass destruction. Now, armed with sling and arrow, axe and spear, a hunter he becomes…and one to fear. With brain to strategise and hands to wield; the fiercest beast, and least, is forced to yield. Hence, in an evolutionary way, in all the animal kingdom Man held sway. Then, not content to rule all living things, he gouged the earth for other offerings of gold and silver, gems and precious stones to add an air of grandeur to his thrones, or use to bribe the gods for sins repented. (*Thus, organised religion was invented.*)

With every age his engineering skill bent forest, mountain, river to his will. His endless greed for water, land and fuel left Nature with no scope for self-renewal. The human race increased in plague proportion without due diligence, or sense of caution. For aeons Earth endured each grave insult, but sickened in the end as a result.

Soon symptoms due to Man, The Engineer, were manifested in the biosphere. The ozone zone's disrupted operation increased the rate of U V radiation and in the oceans dire effects were felt as glaciers and ice-caps start to melt due to the level of the hot-house gases that, year by year, the atmosphere amasses.

On pasturelands, for decades over-grazed, a drought-inducing sun intensely blazed; to make room as huge palm-oil groves appeared rainforest wilderness was quickly cleared. And residues from Man's activities polluted skies and fields and streams and seas, reducing Earth's capacity to feed the masses. Man fell victim to Man's greed.

As nations found themselves in dire peril, the Rule of Law dissolved and they went feral; invading neighbours, greedy for resources, employing all the might of their armed forces. And Man, in spite of his relentless rise, became the agent of his own demise. Until, at length, just scattered tribes remained to count the bitter harvest that they'd gained: despite opposing thumb and cunning brain, reduced to hunter/gatherers again. 'Midst desolation he had brought about, the flame of Mankind flickered…and went out.

And approbation 'round the world was voiced as every other living thing rejoiced. Evolution said "Things didn't go as planned. Henceforth opposing thumbs are strictly banned!"

Speaking in Tongues

I hear that our Prime Minister
Is speaking Mandarin.
He's got our pollies panicky.
He's got them in a spin.
They fear that they'll be left behind,
politic'lly hamstrung,
if they don't get their fingers out
and learn a foreign tongue.

Chorus:

So, sing the National Anthem
and sing it in Chinese.
We're true blue multi-cultural
Australians if you please.

Yes, one is learning Russian,
another modern Greek.
A third aspires to learn the words
all good Norwegians speak.
And one has gone to Pakistan
to visit Rawalpindi.
He claims it on his taxes coz
he's brushing up his Hindi !

Chorus:

So, sing the National Anthem,
yes sing it loud and strong.
If you sing it in Swahili
who'll know if you got it wrong ?

And this one studies Spanish,
another one, Urdu.
When all let go together
it'll be an Irish stew.
But, of course, they've got it all ballsed up,
because there is no sign
that any of that useless mob
can speak in true-blue "Strine".

Chorus:

So, sing the National Anthem,
and belt it out with joy.
In case you 'ave forgot the words,
it's "Aussie, Aussie, Oi ! "

The Snowy Headed Giver

Consternation in the nation
when a rumour went around,
that a whopping great recession's on the way.
And the banks all sang in chorus
"in the red is where we're bound"
and investment comp'nies cried "we cannot pay!"
All the world's big-notes and statesmen
from the countries near and far,
got together to discuss their dreadful plight.
For the big-wigs love a junket
where they have an open bar,
and the pollies blow and prattle with delight.

And one was there, an aussie,
in whom ambition never ceased.
He was something like a Whitlam, undersized.
With a touch of Tintin in him,
three parts unionist at least,
and as such by Labour hacks are highly prized.
But still new to halls of power,
some there wished he'd go away.
"These problems are too much for such as you".
"His policies are bunkum",
we heard Mr Turnbull say,
and Abbot and Costello thought so too.

So he mooched around the edges,
just Obama stood his friend,
"I think we ought to let him have his head.
I warrant he'll be with us
when we want someone to spend,
for both his banks and he are Aussie bred."

"He hails from up in Queensland,
where banana benders bide,
where land and loans are cheap at half the price.
Where a horses hoof 's in danger
from the 'Johs' on every side,
and the pollies are not slow to grab their slice."

"And the Snowy Headed Giver
in that milieu makes his home
where cash in paper bags are passed between;
I have met a fair few pollies
since I moved into the 'Dome',
but nowhere such a spender have I seen."
So he stayed... they found the bourses
round the world were in a slump,
and debated on the way to turn the tide,
and Obama gave his orders,
"We must spend to prime the pump,
it's gunna be a most expensive ride."

"And, Kevin, you must lead them,
spend your surplus left and right.
Spend boldly lad, and never mind the cost.
For never was the stock exchange
in such a dreadful plight,
since the thirties saw so many fortunes lost."
So Kevin spent like fury...
like an heiress on a fling...
like a bold and fearless gambler on a spree.
And he spent his surplus faster,
for the stimulus would bring
a recognition rare for such as he.

"We'll all be rooned" cried Turnbull,
for Pete's sake, rein it in.
"By deficit and taxes we'll be bled."
But 'The Giver' never faltered
as he gave away the tin
and the other punters followed where he led.
With deft, expensive footwork,
he danced round recession's rim,
while keeping unemployment rates at bay.
And Obama and the bankers
rained their praises down on him:
"The Snowy Headed Giver saves the day!"

Now 'The snowy Headed Giver'
has the whole wide world to save
from Climate Change..."While I'm still in my prime."
And Recession's just a mem'ry
and ol' Turnbull's in his grave.
(A week in politic's a long, long time.)

Shortly after these events, as we know, Kevin also received a sharp reminder (between the shoulderblades) that, since Menzies' day, leaders of Australian political parties no longer enjoy tenure (see Julia Seizer and the Mad Abbot next).

Julia Siezer and The Mad Abbot

So we face a new election where, on any fair inspection,
we must choose between assassins, both with blood upon their hands,
who have exercised their power at the mirky midnight hour
to muster mutineers who ride their races in the stands.

And a bloke must stare in wonder at the 'Party Hacks' who blunder
from one leader to another, fearful they might lose their seat.
For their leader's head they're calling if they see the straw-polls falling.
One more empty Pyrric vict'ry; one more doleful, dread retreat.

For the int'rests that are vested pull the reins, but go untested
by the general population, casting their impotent votes.
For 'conglommerated' power makes the politicians cower...
and for cowardice and weakness there are no known antidotes.

So it's 'status quo' dear reader; we've no say in who is leader
(unless you're asked by Gallup Polls which one of two's your choice).
You can make some noisy protest, but you haven't the remotest
chance of being heard by back-room boys...to their ears, we've no voice.

The hung parliament that resulted from this election I think reflects the dilemma I referred to in the introduction to this piece...that of a choice between two equally poor options. Of course, politicians are too removed from reality to comprehend the concept of the grave being a final resting place, so the spectres of Turnbull and Rudd continue to haunt us even today.

The (Modern) Miner's Right

With impugnity I stake my claim
on land held in another's name.
On Liverpool Plains or Liverpool street,
I plant my flag at my neighbour's feet.

(*and I repeat*)

With impugnity I set my drill
to plumb the depths just where I will;
to seek and claim the lion's share
of mineral treasures buried there.

(*and some to spare*)

In governments I place my trust
(*without me budgets would go bust*)
to neither hinder nor impede
my industry with word or *deed.*

(*nor stint my greed*)

Though some who in Suburbia dwell
might get upset, (*so what the hell!*)
their peace and quiet have to go
if there's deposits down below.

(*get with the flow!*)

Opponents say I sacrifice
good farmland at a discount price
and damage aquifers and streams
by tapping into caol gas seams

and (*in their dreams*),

my right to mine should be curtailed.
But that's a plan that's always failed.
While ever there's a need for ore
the Miner's Right is held in awe.

And what is more...

to rein me in they never will,
for if they introduce a bill
to increase taxes that I pay
(*I rarely pay them anyway*)

well, I just say....

"We'll have to close down mines and all
employees' rates will have to fall!
Ten thousand jobs will have to go!
It's fiscal suicide, you know!"

(*though it ain't so*)

And if they try to bung a tax
on carbon wafting up the stacks
of customers that I sell to,
(*don't let on I'm the one told you*)

here's what I do...

I weep and wail: "The sky will fall!
You'll send my business to the wall!
A *hundred* thousand jobs will go!"
AND MOST BELIEVE ME, don'cha know!

(*ho, ho, ho, ho*)

So journos then attack the tax
and, backed by Opposition hacks,
they fan the flame and light the fuse
that blows up on the evening news.

And all accuse

supporters of this horrid bill
of trying industry to kill.
and irresponsibility
in framing fiscal policy...

and me?...still free

to rape the land; pollute the soil;
spoil water in pursuit of oil;
trash people's lives in search of gold
and gas and coalfields, new or old.

.............And so, behold!

The Miner's Right! The right that bends
all others' rights to my own ends;
to plunder more and render less;
make heaps from pits and leave a mess.

(*and YOU acquiesce?*)

Blended Spirits

When the Spirit of Forgiveness
meets the Spirit of Regret,
recognising we are one beneath the skin;
putting past mistakes behind us
and a new example set,
then reconciliation can begin.

Where the Spirits of the Future
and Tradition intersect
(the child is born of those who've gone before);
when the Spirit of Acceptance
builds a Culture of Respect,
a new and brighter future lies in store.

When the Spirit of our Country
is a blend of old and new,
past prejudice and hatreds cast aside;
when Kindness and Compassion
count among her retinue,
we'll justify our patriotic pride.

The Great Australian Hole

This country needs a 'gee-up'...an inspiring common cause.
A project like The Snowy Scheme that won so much applause.
Some challenge to unite us all to work toward some goal...
and since you ask, well I suggest ...'The Great Australian Hole'.

Now, BHP and Fortescue have made a damned good start,
but now it's time the rest of us pitched in and did our part.
We'll simply dig the whole lot out and auction off the best,
then build a causeway down to the Antarctic with the rest.

We're worried by the changes that this 'Climate Change' will bring.
"How can our big hole help with that?" you ask...well, here's the thing.
We build a great big pipeline where our causeway bridge will be,
then pump the melting ice-cap, and create an inland sea!

This fabled Inland Sea all those explorers failed to find
will lie resplendent in the hole from all the ore we've mined.
All round the rim we'll leave a bit of decent high, dry land
and lots of islands in the sea with fringing reefs and sand.

Resorts and swish marinas will spring up round Uluru...
(we'll plant a lot of palm trees there and call it 'Hula-Roo').
Big regattas will be sailing right across the One Tree Plain
(but four-wheel drives will never cross the Nullabor again!)

"But what about the landscape round the Corner Country pegs?"
Well, if you want an omelette mate, you have to break some eggs.
"And what about the wombats? What about the Kangaroos?"
Well, that's the price you have to pay for homes with water views.

This Inland Archipelago will be a wondrous thing ;
what's lost upon the roundabout, we'll pick up on the swing.
The Treasury will benefit, of that there is no doubt.
No longer will they subsidise poor farmers hit by drought.

The farmers and the graziers will have to be re-trained
to gather in the harvest from the fishing grounds we've gained.
All the billions that it cost will seem a piffling amount
when the flood of tourist dollars fill up every bank account.

And Canberra? It's just the place for all the watery graves
of all those politicians who have sunk beneath the waves.
And all who love Australia will be thankful to a man.
The Great Hole Of Australia ! What a bold and brilliant plan.

Muted Joy

Our church has had a lick of paint.
My word, it's looking dapper.
But the old church-bell is impotent
because it's lost its clapper.

The 'noise abatement' rules enforced
by councilmen and mayor
decree no more the bell shall call
the faithful down to prayer.

No more shall wedding bells ring out
for happy bride and groom.
Midst traffic's roar and beat-box blare,
for chimes there is no room.

At Easter and at Christmas-tide
no carillons rejoice.
Because bureaucracy's gone mad,
our church has lost its voice.

Your anguished protests count for nought:
the law we must obey.
Church-bells shall henceforth silent be.
(that is, 'til Judgement Day).

Moderation

I wonder if the human race will ever overcome
the penchant for extremist views exhibited by some ?
Whatever ideology or issue is at stake,
there's always a fanatic fringe with mad demands to make.
There's differing opinions on the left and on the right,
and those who take the middle ground get swept up in the fight.
The voice of moderation's often drowned out in the fray.
There's always those who disagree with everything you say.

It must be in their nature for some folk to fight it seems;
to always take the selfish course and trample others' dreams.
Without a care or caution for the other fellow's plight,
insisting on the lion's share they claim is theirs by right.
Afflicted with a jaundiced mind, their grievances abound,
rejecting every overture to find some common ground.
Oh, give me moderation, may it reign above all things
and save us from the mayhem that fanaticism brings.

Section 7

Around the Towns

Albury - Wodonga

Oh I'd love to linger longer
in the township of Wodonga
but Albury my home is calling me.
Though I'm filled with admiration
for Wodonga's situation,
still, my heart says "Head back home to Albury."

Oh, it's goodbye to old Wodonga,
I can't stay a moment longer...
for I'm on my way back home
to New South Wales.

Yes, I have to make that journey
cross the Murray, wet and ferny,
coz I'm homesick for my home in New South Wales.
Though Wodonga is attractive,
she can't keep this cornstalk captive,
coz my love for my old hometown never fails.

Oh, it's goodbye to old Wodonga,
there's a place for which I hunger
and I'm making my way home
to New South Wales.

So I'll set out in the morning,
though the locals here are warning
of the perils of the trip, I'll take a stab.
Take that long road set before me...
mind you, if the skies turn stormy,
I might have to change my plans and take a cab.

Yes, goodbye dear old Wodonga,
there's a place whose draw is stronger...
and there's no place quite like home
in New South Wales.

The Ridge

If you go to Lightening Ridge, well, you just might need a fridge
if your plans include at night a spot of sleepin'.
It might help to keep you cool and might go some way to fool
all the scorpians and snakes that come a'creepin'.

If you think White Cliffs is hot and you think the Ridge is not,
let me tell ya mate, it isn't that much colder.
There's a way the locals know the temp is forty or below:
when it's forty plus, the mullock starts to smoulder.

Locals will agree I think that they're partial to a drink
whether down below or up above ground level.
Where a keg is to be found they will all be gathered 'round...
that's why their cuts have always got a bevel.

Once they took a census there (this is ridgy-didge, I swear)
and the result said only "Population : floating."
Well that may be true although, what I'd really like to know,
where the heck is this big pond where they go boating ?

If you're up in Lightening Ridge just ask Mack or Mick or Midge
if you're looking for a little satisfaction.
They will tell you "Day or night, if you have a Miner's Right,
underground's the only place to find the action."

But then if you just can't stand all that heat and dust and sand,
and if bush flies in their multitudes repel you,
you're in luck! I've got a stock of some really high grade rock,
if you're interested mate, that I can sell you.

<u>Crook-Well ?</u>

Well, here we are in Crookwell
and, by gee, I think it's crook
that you never know in Crookwell
whether things are well or crook!

Yes, things are crook in Crookwell,
half the town at least is crook.
But the townsfolk here in Crookwell,
well, it's strange how well they look.

It's hard to tell in Crookwell
who's a real good Crookwell cook.
Though their dishes may be cooked well,
they may make you feel...well...crook.

Yes, here we are in Crookwell,
and crook crooks must think it's swell
that there's such a place as Crookwell
where a crook crook can get well.

Now, water here in Crookwell
surely must come from that well.
But I wouldn't drink the water...
it might make you feel unwell.

So, if you come to Crookwell
mark my words and mark them well,
drink the beer...it's swell in Crookwell,
but don't drink from Crookwell's well.

Broke

Introduction

With apologies to the good citizens of the real town of Broke. Any similarity to any person, living or dead, and/or their economic status is purely imaginary.

There's a little town called Broke on the Hunter Valley's rim,
and as the town's name would imply, things there are pretty grim.
They haven't got a brass razoo, they haven't got a penny.
Their goods and chattels very few. In fact, they haven't any.

They can't afford a country pub, they can't afford a hall.
They have no use for telephones; they can't afford the call.
They can't afford a sporting ground on which a bloke might camp.
They have no need of mailmen, coz they can't afford a stamp.

They once had a game of footy, with a pumpkin for a ball.
The ref, he had no whistle, so they couldn't hear his call.
They wound up with a pumpkin mash each time they had a maul.
The match was called because of soup and ended in a brawl.

Their clothes are made of hessian, so they very seldom grin.
To waste their breath upon a laugh, to them would be a sin.
The local Swimming Centre is a rusty water tank.
The parson's empty poor-box doubles as the local bank.

They can't afford a church although they are religious people.
They found a broken Comet 'mill and use that for a steeple.
They can't afford to sit inside on proper oaken pews,
and so they perch on fallen logs to hear the parson's views.

And when he sends the plate around on Sundays there in Broke,
he's lucky if he gets it back, with just a lump of coke.
A proper funeral costs too much. Blokes can't afford a bride.
So no-one there has ever wed, and none of them has died !

P.S.

If it happens you're a person that's residing in this town,
I hope my little poem didn't give you cause to frown.
It's just a little fun you know, that I could not resist,
when I saw "Broke, 2330" there on my postcode list.

I hope you take it in good part, I don't mean to offend.
Believe me when I tell you that's the last thing I intend.
But if it made you angry, then please blame the fellow who
bequeathed your town its pauper's name, and left it haunting you.

P.P.S.

I heard there was another town, if rumour can be trusted,
a little down the road from yours. He planned to call it **"Busted".**
To cap it all, a third was planned, and they would all be clustered
close together on the map: **"Broke", "Busted" and "Disgusted" !**

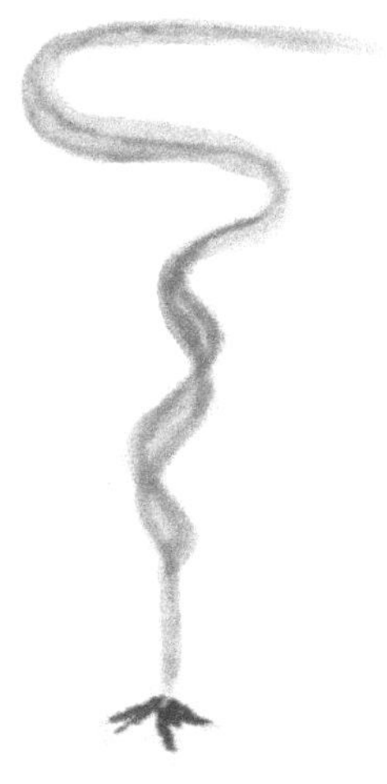

Dunedoo

How did Dunedoo get famous?
I might be an ignoramus
but it seems to me the name provides the clue.
For it can't be for its glamour
that the visitors all clamour...
no, it's just to say "We've been to Dunedoo."

There are lots of towns frequented
by the caravanned and tented,
with a lot of things to see and things to do.
They've attractions much, much bigger
and the townsfolk there would snigger
if you dared they be compared to Dunedoo.

It can't be for their museum
that the people come to see 'em...
every self-respecting township has one too.
And there's lots of country places
that have Balls and Picnic Races
that are bigger than the balls of Dunedoo.

They have Festivals of Music
of the country style acoustic;
as for Rodeos, you'll find that there's a slew.
Heaven knows they're not that wealthy.
I don't think it's coz it's healthy...
there are lots of towns more flush than Dunedoo.

Now it may be just a rumour,
but they say that it's the humour
in the name that brings such fame to Dunedoo.
I suppose some find it funny
to make silly rhymes with 'dunny'...
don't ask me! It's something I would *never* do!

Gunnedah

You can drive your car out to Gunnedah
if the roads are fit to travel.
For the fearless few, motorbikes will do
if you look out for the gravel.
If you own a horse, you can ride of course,
if you're easy in the saddle.
With a flood or two and a good canoe
you may get there if you paddle.

You can go by train, you can hire a plane
or, with Greyhound, you can coach it.
By a dozen roads and by diverse modes
are the ways you can approach it.
If you like, hitch-hike...you can ride your bike,
if you own a Malvern Star.
But you *must not* walk - that's just crazy talk -
Mate, it's just too flamin' far!

Section 8

<u>*For the Diggers*</u>

Dawn Service

"I'll meet you at the cenotaph at dawn on Anzac Day."
The blokes from my battalion...every year, that's what we say.
We share a minute's silence there, and then recite The Ode.
Recalling mates, forever young, and the debt that's owed.

Then later on we muster ranks to march along the street
with military bands to spur on old and feeble feet.
The crowds will cheer as ever and they'll keep us going strong...
all smiling, waving...weeping...as each unit stumps along.

And filling out our ranks there'll be some there who are too young
to know the horrors seen by we old men they march among.
They're marching for the honour of their father's father's name.
Though missing from their unit's ranks, remembered just the same.

For every year among us march the ever-growing hosts
of those… "The Unforgotten"...our unseen comrades' ghosts.
Already gone the diggers who had fought in The Great War
and soon will all the veterens of The Second be no more.

Though time must take its toll on us, until we all are gone,
that bond that's bound us all these years, I'm certain, will live on.
And ever shall my spirit come, though life be sped away...
"I'll meet you at the cenotaph...at dawn...on Anzac Day."

This Anzac Day in the year 2010, for the first time since their tragic deaths in the battle at Fromelles in France in World War 1, the British and Australian soldiers who were buried in mass graves in a field in Pheasant Wood will lie at rest in a properly consecrated war cemetery, having been re-interred with full military honours.

Fromelles: Missing, Unaccounted For

Here again, in Pheasant Wood, the snow lies all around
and paints with cool white purity the blood soaked battle ground
as it has done, each winter past, these ninety lonely years.
Yet still it has not healed the soil, nor dried the ghostly tears
of those who sleep here 'neath its shroud, unshriven and alone.
Two hundred fifty men here still...but whereabouts "unknown".
Two fifty victims of the blast of bomb and mortar shells.
Two fifty unaccounted from the hell that was Fromelles.

These young men, uncomplaining, went with courage to the fight,
believing in their youthful hearts their cause was just and right.
And in these fields the thousands died, while inept generals stood
in bunkers safe and snug...and far removed from Pheasant Wood.
A fearful toll was levied by machine gun enfilade.
In spite of all their sacrifice, no gain in ground was made.
Regardless of the trauma to the shell-shocked men they led,
the British High Command refused a truce to clear their dead.

Heroic deeds of daring under cover of the night
were carried out by Diggers, who knew it wasn't right
to leave their fallen mates out there, alone in No Man's Land,
and disregarded orders that they couldn't understand.
All through the hours of darkness, risking injury and death,
they sought to find the fallen and the mates who still drew breath.
In spite of their cool gallantry, the numbers were too great.
With bitter grief they had to leave too many to their fate.

The enemy consigned their broken bodies to the earth
in mass graves in a foreign field, far from their land of birth.
Then, with the passing of the years, the memory of this place
where lie the lost two fifty faded, almost beyond trace.
And if we do not mention here all those (though they don't ask
for praise or recognition) who have bent upon this task
their strength and dedication to reclaim them from the past,
they saw and did their duty, and they found their graves at last.

Now here in Pheasant Wood again, the snow lies all around.
Beneath its muted mantle, newly consecrated ground.
With military honours now, the lost from the 'Great War'
receive their fitting resting place "Present...and accounted for."

Re-Dedication *Introduction*

Yesterday, 24th November 2009, saw the re-dedication of the War Memorial in Hyde Park, Sydney after extensive repairs and re-furbishment on the 75th anniversary of its opening. The memorial is an imposing example of Art Deco monumental architecture incorporating a number of striking features. In particular, the beautiful Pool of Reflection fronting the monument, the imposing bulk of the building itself, and inside, the Well of Contemplation which is a gallery overlooking a confronting but impressive sculpture of a dead youth borne on a shield which is itself supported on the shoulders of three women. These represent the grieving loved ones left behind. The memorial was dedicated to all those volunteers from NSW who fought in the 'Great War'.

Re-Dedication

In the midst of a great city, near its hard and harried heart,
lies a green and leafy refuge that our forebears set apart.
On its lawns and in its bowers, as the work-day's cares increase,
one can find a welcome respite; one can find a moment's peace.

At the far end of this parkland stands a monument to war.
But the pilgrim's not mistaken, for that's not what it stands for.
By the pool he may reflect on the futility of war,
then approach the Bathurst granite by the broad stairs at its shore.

Rising battlements are guarded by stern figures, circumspect,
contemplating on lost comrades and commanding our respect.
Step inside the Hall of Mem'ry, there you'll see the sacred flame.
It's a flame that burns eternal, and Remembrance is it's name.

For each volunteer who rallied in defence of freedom's cause,
on the ceiling you will see stars. 'Twas the 'War to end all wars'.
Now look down upon the figure of the young man crucified,
laid upon the shield of battle, sacrificed and sanctified.

See the burden borne by women. See the mother, daughter, wife.
See the grief and bitter harvest reaped from warfare's angry strife.
You look down upon this vision of the awful cost of war;
contemplating with your head bowed, what has all this pain been for?

Think about the men and women who have fought and served since then
in the wars and bitter conflicts that erupt time and again.
But, alas, it's human nature that when Freedom's threatened by
some mad despot or fanatic, then good men must fight and die.

By the Well of Contemplation, in the silence we reflect,
sometimes Freedom's price is more than our good-will or intellect.
So then let us all remember, at sunrise and at sunset,
there's a price to peace and freedom. Paid by them.
...Lest We Forget.

Reflections on Anzac Day

Yesterday

In righteous indignation, or to even up a score,
with patriotic fervour, angry nations go to war.
The war cry and the call to arms demand we don't think twice
to offer up our nation's youth in bloody sacrifice.
At length the strife is over and the task at last is done.
Bereft of doting father, of a husband or a son,
all the children, all the widows, all the mothers left to weep,
must struggle on without their men, forevermore asleep.

Today

Each year they muster in the dawn. The bugler sounds Last Post.
Each year the oath, 'Lest We Forget', intoned from coast to coast.
Each year we see the Diggers march, each year their ranks deplete.
Those Warfare could not overcome, by Time at last are beat.
Each year we see less Diggers march, each year so swift in flight.
Each year the comrades that remain "Close ranks, dress by the right".
Each year the memories flood back and make our hearts recoil
for all their brother Southern Sons, asleep neath foreign soil.

Tomorrow ?

These swords and battle standards, relics of another age,
before the human race had learned to close the blood-stained page
on wars and racial hatred that once tore our world apart,
remind us all that savagery lurks in the human heart.
These cenotaphs and war graves are reminders of the cost.
If we fail to heed their warnings, then the human race is lost.
With thankful heart and sober mind we pledge that we'll maintain
a world in which our children never go to war again.

"Those heroes that shed their blood and lost their lives, you are now lying in the soil of a friendly country. Therefore, rest in peace.

There is no difference between the Johnnies and the Mehmets to us where they lie, side by side, here in this country of ours.

You, the mothers who sent their sons from far away countries, wipe away your tears. Your sons are now lying in our bosom, and are at peace. After having lost their lives on this land, they have become our sons as well."

Mustafa Kamal Attaturk

Brothers in Arms

Brother, do you remember
on these wild and stony slopes,
how we fought with fire and fury
to fulfil our generals' hopes...?

how we strove with gun and bayonet...
with grenade and mortar too...
do you recall the scream of shellfire
and the shrapnel shards that flew...?

the deadly frenzied rushes,
trench to trench across Lone Pine...
the desperation of the battle
to dig in and hold the line...?

and brother, do you remember,
all our comrades who were slain
and the anguish of the wounded
crying out in fear and pain...?

And Mehmet, do you remember,
what our sacrifice was for...
do you understand the reasons
our two countries were at war...?

....Never mind. The war is over.
The sounds of battle cease.
The sun sets over Anzac Cove...
let us, brother, rest in peace.

Section 9

Life's Like That

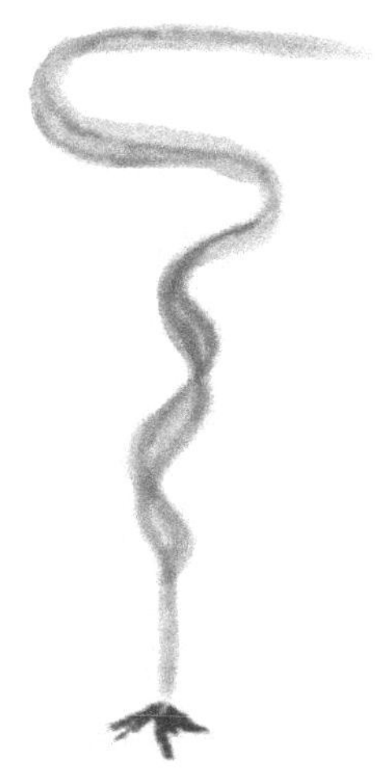

It Wasn't Me!

It wasn't me what dunnit:
I shouldn' get tha blame.
Another kid just blew 'is lid
because 'e lost the game!

It wasn't me what dunnit;
I didn't chuck the stone.
It just ain't fair for me to bear
the blame all on me own!

It wasn't me what dunnit;
I shouldn' get the strap.
An' please don't shout, just hear me out,
it was the other chap.

I know the kid what done it.
He's always in the stew.
But here's the hitch...I'd be a snitch
to tell 'is name to you.

It wasn't me what dunnit;
'tain't fair that I'm the one
who's bum is sore in payment for
what Jimmy Wilson done!

Cryin' In Me Beer

Cryin' in me beer,
I'm cryin' in me beer.
My story's sad, so lend an ear
I'm cryin' in me beer.

Luck's a fortune, so they say,
but none 'as ever come my way.
I've never 'ad a lucky day...
I'm cryin' in me beer.

Cryin' in me beer,
I'm cryin' in me beer.
Gawd struth, it's been a lousy year,
I'm cryin' in me beer.

At ev'ry opportunity
Lady Luck 'as turned on me
an' blighted me with poverty...
I'm cryin' in me beer.

Cryin' in me beer,
me rent is in arrears.
I'm drinkin' shandies, cut with tears,
from cryin' in me beer.

I could 'ave been a prosp'rous bloke,
but when a chance would come I'd choke
an' wind up down an' out flat broke...
'an cryin' in me beer.

Cryin' in me beer,
me wife is such a dear...
she's chucked out all me fishin' gear...
I'm cryin' in me beer.

I bet the fav'rite yesterday
an' gave the bookies all me pay.
Damned nag took off the other way!
I'm cryin' in me beer.

Cryin' in me beer,
I've done me dash, it's clear.
Declare a war, I'll volunteer!
I'm cryin' in me beer.

It ain' t that I ain't got the nouse
to keep a job an' buy a house.
But ev'ry boss I've 'ad's a louse.
I'm cryin' in me beer.

Cryin' in me beer,
I've made it my career.
From nine to five you'll find me here
just cryin' in me beer.

It's not my fault, I'm not to blame.
There's lots of causes I could name,
an' puntin' is a funny game...
I'm cryin' in me beer.

Cryin' in me beer,
'an feelin 'rather queer.
I'm not long for this world I fear!
I'm cryin' in me beer.

<u>Born to be Blue</u>

In Queensland to help all their sugarcane grow
they let loose some cane-toads to see how they'd go.
In canefields they were not content to reside...
like fleas on a dog, they soon spread far and wide.
Quickly becoming the world's greatest pest,
they bred just like flies in the North and the West.
But here in the South where they thought to expand,
the almighty Blues drew a line in the sand.

Born to be Blue, Born to be Blue.
In NSW we are blue through and through.
Cane-toads, the true-blues are gunning for you,
In New SouthWales, we were born to be blue!

The cane toads were many, their skin it was it was rough,
but in New South Wales, we are bred to be tough...
the honour of New South Wales ours to defend.
We're born to be blue and we'll fight to the end.

Born to be Blue, Born to be Blue.
They call us cockroaches and other things too.
But we are the Cornstalks, the great chosen few...
In New SouthWales, we were born to be blue!

Sometimes there was glory, at times it was hell
and many the heroes that rose and that fell.
Whatever the outcome of battle we knew,
we'd given our all in defence of the Blue.

Born to be Blue, Born to be Blue.
Bugger the odds, NSW are tru-blue.
Stand by your team-mates, whatever you do.
Go NSW, boys we're counting on you .

Born to be Blue, Born to be Blue.
In NSW we are blue through and through.
Stand by your team-mates, whatever you do.
Go NSW, we were born to be blue!

The Fading Of The Light

On a good day he remembers
and can speak with me by name;
we can have a conversation...
but no two days are the same.
On those days he doesn't know me,
I just tell him "It's alright."
Then we sit and wait together,
for the coming of the night.

He can reminisce in detail
on those days when he was small,
with a sort of anxious passion
and with crystal clear recall.
But reminding him of something
that we spoke about last night,
in his eyes I see confusion...
and a fading of the light.

Once those eyes were lit with kindness
and with humour sparkled bright.
Now a shadow grows within them
as dementia starts to bite.
What a cruel fate to suffer
and for me, a hateful sight...
to become a helpless witness
to the fading of the light.

Terms Of Trade

Ya think coz I'm a Tradie, ya can take the blanky Mick!
Tha crook wrap that we Tradies cop, fair dinkum, makes me sick.
Ya whinge that it's too early if ya first job out tha gate,
but ya reckon you been got at if we lob at five past eight.

"Now mind ya wipe ya muddy boots, and clean up when ya done"
Life as a flamin' Tradie, I can tell ya, ain't much fun.
It's yoosherly you housewives is tha ones 'oo wanna mag,
or launch into a leksha every time ya lights a fag.

Yoo'll spend a blanky forchoon on a tub a wrinkle goo,
but squeal like 'bloody murder' when I 'ands me bill to you.
When ya ask me " 'Ow ya goin' ?", it's a pretty certain bet
that tha thing yer really thinkin' is : "Gawd, aincha finished yet?"

Lantana

The experts say lantana
is just a weed that's vile,
and say it has no virtues,
and on it scorn they pile.
I say we should consider:
its flowers are very cute.
For being multi-coloured
they have no substitute.
They're robust and they're hardy;
they're green throughout the year.
They need no fertilizing
or care to grow, that's clear.
Drought only seems to suit them.
They thrive with vim and vigour.
Prune lightly to a stump and they
will soon be four times bigger.
They sprout in all directions
from twig or leaf with zest.........
Go get my saw and mattock dear;
this thing's a god-damned pest!

Brookie Show

Remember how we used to go to the Brookie Show each year ?
(Through a gap in the chainwire fence, as soon as the coast was clear.)
The entry fee was better spent on rides and stalls and stuff.
The dodg'em cars, the Octopus...we couldn't get enough.

Remember how they used to have a dirt track round the ring ?
And once a year we'd get to cheer the harness racing king.
The pounding hooves would thunder by and whip-cracks fill the air,
as they hurtled round inside the fence with scarce an inch to spare.

And gawking at the side-show girls, clad in their clinging togs.
Spangles flashing in the lights...we hopped around like frogs
to try and get a better view between the grown-ups there.
Us little kids had never seen such glamour anywhere.

And Sharman had that boxing tent; he'd always get a few
to have a go and see if they could last a round or two.
Few ever made it to the bell or went home with a purse.
They mostly got a lesson, and a bruise or two to nurse.

The moving target shooting stall, no chance we'd pass that by.
"Two bob, ten shots". We'd lay it down and let the pellets fly.
The "dazzling prizes" up for grabs, if eye and luck were in ?
A cheap and nasty Cupie-Doll ! ..straight in the rubbish bin !

The soggy chips, the fairy floss and luke-warm fizzy drinks.
After a ride on the "CHA-CHA-CHA", a lot went down the sinks.
Our pocket money soon ran out and, nothing left to spend,
we'd mooch around on weary legs until the very end.

And then we'd drag ourselves back home, collapse into our beds.
The sights and sounds of Brookie Show still ringing in our heads.

The View From Room 7

Within these antiseptic walls they keep me clothed and fed;
but I wouldn't call this living, I might just as well be dead.
A long and rugged life has left me with a shrivelled shell.
My body might be broken but my mind's clear as a bell.

Because I can't communicate, they treat me like a child;
a misdirected letter, I've been sorted, stamped and filed.
I've nothing now but memories to get me through each day.
They tend to my frail body while my mind is far away.

A sea of roofs and street lamps lie beyond this window sill,
but 'though I may not see them, there are trees beyond that hill.
'Cause when the breeze is blowing right it carries me their smell;
the sweet scent of the eucalypt that I love oh, so well.

It's that special smell of gum leaves that carries me away
to another place, another time, before my hair was grey.
My back was strong, my wind was sound and I was clear of eye,
when I, a lad of eighteen years, left home in Mungindi.

Taking work where I could find it, I learned how to earn a crust;
'cause when you hump your bluey, you must take each day on trust.
There's always work for good hands who are game to have a go.
Just down the road might be a job, with luck, you never know.

I've laboured in the wheat fields and I've worked with sheep and beef.
I've worked with lots of good blokes and with some who gave me grief.
In hard times I've met some who'd give the shirt right off their back.
I've met them all and left them...far behind me down the track.

There was a time I thought that I should maybe settle down,
to live like normal people, with a wife and kids in town.
But soon enough the open road was calling out to me.
"Pull up the stakes and go" became my one philosophy.

Down through the years I must have tramped ten thousand miles or more
and tried my hand at every job there is within the law.
I've branded on the high plains and built bridges over creeks;
checked corner country fences and seen not a soul in weeks.

I've camped among the mountain ash, by streams so clear and sweet;
I've shivered in the freezing night and sweltered in the heat.
Watched sunsets paint the Flinders Range, the Paroo flood the plain;
Seen moonlight on Menindee Lakes. Sights I won't see again.

I wouldn't swap the life I've lived, now coming to its end.
Been stuck in this damn place too long...
time to see what's round the bend.

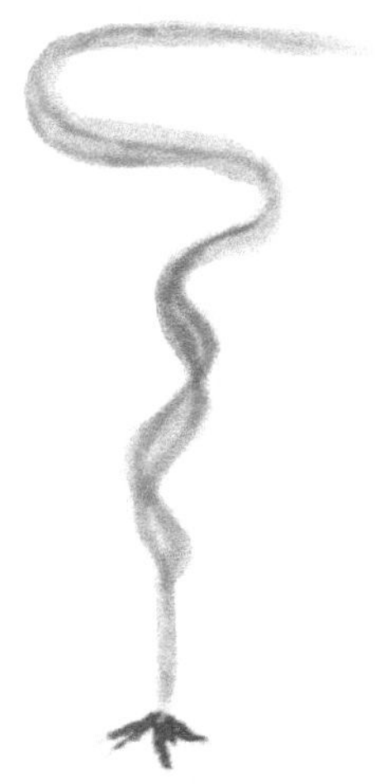

Out Of Order

(or "Where Do Ya Get It ?" A One Act Play Of Indeterminate Length)

I went to my fav'rite chinese caf' last night to get a feed,
but when we saw the menu my taste buds and I agreed
that we weren't in the mood tonight for curried prawns and rice,
and then we both decided that lasagne would be nice.

I called the waiter over and said "When you have a mo',
I'm ready now to order and lasagne is the go."
He blinked at me a moment, then he smiled and scratched his head.
"I think that I mis-heard you. Please repeat what you just said."

"A nice dish of lasagne is what I wish to be fed,
and by the way, I'm rather tired of gold and black and red.
This chinese decor clashes with fine Middle Med cuisine.
A dimly lighted grotto would be nice, in shades of green."

The waiter looked askance at me and offered this advice :
"Luigi's Place, just down the street, I hear is very nice.
Their specialty's Italian, if it's pasta you desire.
I'm sorry sir, we can't provide the fare that you require"

I got a little upset, and I said "Now listen here.
I'm a flamin' paying customer. I think it's very queer
I can't go to a restaurant and order what I like,
for if I do, I get from you "Push off! Get on your bike'!"

"I don't mean to offend you sir," he said "or cause you pain,
but we're a Chinese cafe as the menu makes quite plain."
"Chinese is fine from time to time," I said "when in the mood,
but now and then it's good to try another culture's food.

The style of cooking of your chef, (a fact that must be faced)
must catch up with the times and meet my multi-cultured taste."
Just then another patron said "You know, you may be right,
and now I think about it, I'd like Mexican tonight."

Another fellow piped up then and stated with much verve,
"You're causing a commotion mate, I think you've got a nerve
to make a flamin' ruckus and to argue to and fro.
If lasagne's what you're wanting, mate, *I'll* tell you where to go!"

And this went on for hours on end, we argued back and forth.
Some trains of thought were Southward bound while others
headed North.
At last I left there, tired and weak and took a cab back home.
Had vegemite on toast for tea and ice cream (honeycomb).

I think I've learned my lesson though. I'll go back there tonight.
Although I'll be, when they see me, a less than welcome sight.
I'll tell the waiter "My good man, I won't hold up the queue.
I know lasagne's not on, so, I'll just have Irish Stew".

Ballad of the Grey Nomads

Grey Nomads throng the nation's roads all heading where it's sunny.
We've left behind our fixed abode and spending our kids' money.
So load the caravan up mum, we've waited for this day.
Look out Australia, here we come, we are the Nomads Grey !

We'll nip across the Nullabor and see the Southern Ocean.
Come on, what are we waiting for? Let's get these wheels in motion !
A month or so at Kakadu by way of Oodnadatta.
Then Alice for a week or two, to catch the Todd Regatta.

We'll endure a White Cliffs stinker, and we'll eat bush tucker food.
Buy beer at Innaminka, if we're out of our home-brewed.
Watch sunsets on the Timor Sea, moonshine on Arafura.
At harvest time, if you agree, pick fruit down in Mildura.

And everywhere we go we'll meet with members of our band.
The 'Old and Bold' with itchy feet, criss-crossing this great land.
So, load the caravan up and we'll soon be on our way.
Look out Australia, here we come, we are the Nomads Grey !

The open road is calling, there's no reason for delay !
Grey Nomads 'neath the Southern Cross
and WE HAVE RIGHT OF WAY !

Spider, Spider

Spider, spider hanging right
above the place I sleep at night,
think you that I don't see you there
in hopes to catch me unaware
in underwear?

Eight ugly legs and four eyes too,
you horrid hairy creature you!
The alien race from which you come
upsets my equilibrium,
chum.

I s'pose the only thing to do
is introduce you to my shoe.
Then I'll enjoy my peaceful rest
because I know that you're 'depressed'.
Pest!

(I hate spiders!)

A Drowse

It's somewhat lazy I suppose...
to take my ease in sweet repose...
to sip my drink and scratch my nose...

with lawns in need of mowing...

But...

A summer breeze's whisper blows
and bids my listless eyelids close...
and blows a kiss before it goes...

and all the world is slowing...

Annual Report

The fiscal year has come and gone,
Lord knows, how quick it went!
I'm sure you would have noticed,
if a notice had been sent.
But we couldn't spare the money,
'cause the budget was all spent,
and we couldn't spare the paper.
We'd invested every cent.

We've examined every column
in the ledgers and it's clear,
for our directors' bonuses
it's been a bumper year.
But on the other hand it seems
from losses we've incurred,
alas, shareholders' dividends
this year will be deferred.

.....ooo0ooo.....

Unroadworthy

It soon will be my birthday, I'll be turning sixty five.
My make and model's getting rare. At least I still can drive.
Transmission's getting iffy, my suspension's lost its spring;
exhaust won't pass emissions. (think I might have blown a ring.)
My upholstery's rather shabby, and my lights are getting dim;
My big-end's getting flabby and the body's lost some trim.
My steering's got the wobbles, and I go...in fits...and starts.
I tried to get a tune-up but, "ya just can't get the parts".
My running costs are out of hand, I'm always out of cash.
The cooling system's leaky, and my dashboard's done its dash.
I used to zoom in overdrive (to catch up with a Mini.)
but now my valves're rusty, and my horn's a wee bit tinny.
I'm tired of all those up-hill climbs, and done with rego checkers.
From here on in it's all downhill, so point me to the wreckers.

.....ooo0ooo.....

When I Die

How will I,
when I die,
in my head,
know I'm dead ?
It's scarcely sane
without a brain
to be aware
of lack of air!

Section 10

A Motley Mob

Hard a' Hearin'

We're sittin' round the fire one night, each deep in meditation.
An old hand cursed, then turned and said by way of explantion...
"Me father was a Kiwi see? Came over for the shearin'.
Me mother was a Irish girl, and both were hard a' hearin'.

I was just a kid. One day, when Dad gets back to camp
'twas gettin' on to dark, so Mum says " Dad dear, light the lamp".
"the firewood is quite damp" my Dad, mishearin', thought she said.
So Dad he mutters "must I cut some firewood 'fore I'm fed ?"

"Now look you here, my Maori Boy, I only want some light!"
But he heard "Look out boyo, 'coz I'm spoilin' for a fight".
Dad then says "steady on old girl, no need for chuckin' fits"
She thinks he says " don't act the churl, don't give a man the ......
Tom Tits"

So on all through the ruddy night they went with hammer and tong.
No matter what the one would say, the other got it wrong.
An' ev'ry night was much the same, each one misunderstood
the other. But, when neither spoke they got on pretty good!

If only with the hearin' aids, my parents had been fitted,
P'r'aps they'd be together still, but they weren't, and so they splitted."

The Ballad Of Tom Kruze (b. 1914 d. 2011)

There's a bloke who was a legend to some people, so I'm told,
and they reckon when they made Tom Kruze, they threw away the mould.
If you're thinking of that other Tom, you've taken the wrong tack.
This Tom Kruze, he was the Mailman on the barren Birdsville Track.

As the Thirties and the Forties and the Fifties came and went,
in that unforgiving country almost half his life was spent
carting mail and food and fuel, six days there and six days back,
in a battered Leyland Badger down the long, dry Birdsville Track.

Between Marree, South Australia and that Queensland border town,
it was mostly sand and saltbush; dust and dirt of red and brown.
Seven hundred miles of gibbers with huge sand dunes now and then,
there and back the mailman travelled...and then did it all again.

To the people who were strewn along the distance in between,
as he followed in the faint tracks where the camel teams had been,
he became a vital life-line to the world beyond their gates
bearing news and fuel and letters stacked up high in drums and crates.

Miles and miles away from nowhere, scorched by day and chilled by night...
where a drover with some cattle was a rare and welcome sight...
in that god-forsaken landscape, nary shanty, shed nor shack,
year on endless year he battled with that blasted Birdsville Track.

Blinding heat and stoney stretches, wild dust storms and flooded creeks,
busted spring or broken axle, could maroon him there for weeks.
If the poor old Badger's tailshaft took a really solid whack,
it was hoof it out or fix it on that fearsome Birdsville Track.

Two years straight the Cooper flooded causing old Tom lots of pain,
punting cargo cross the water...then re-loading it again
on another of his lorries waiting on the other side.
Month on weary month repeated 'til the turgid waters dried.

But Tom Kruze, he had a contract to make sure the mail went through;
camping rough and mostly barefoot, doing what he had to do.
Whether inching over sandhills in fierce, unrelenting heat
or digging out of boggy ground, old Tom was never beat.

In Nineteen Fifty Four, Tom Kruze's fame was spread afar...
Tom Kruze The Birdsville Mailman had became a movie star.
And for all his years of service between Birdsville and Marree,
in Nineteen Fifty Five the Queen gave Tom an MBE.

So, this postie now was legend far beyond his outback beat
and a truer, dinkum battler you could never hope to meet.
Outback characters are many...one stands out amongst the pack.
Old Tom Kruze, the Barefoot Mailman of the barren Birdsville Track.

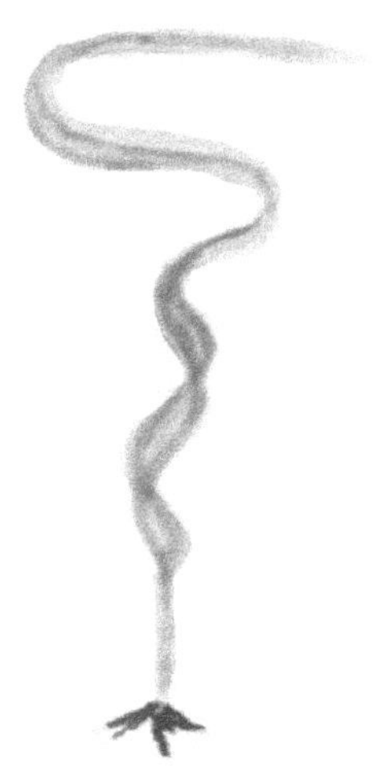

Order Of Service

When my time comes, if you're a mate,
put wattle on me grave.
Don't sing some sorry fun'ral dirge,
that's no way to behave.
Don't dress me in a poncie suit
(I always was a dag).
Don't put me in a wooden box,
just wrap me in me swag.

Make sure that there's some gum trees near
to shade me from the heat.
I still might get the wanders,
so put 'Bluchers' on me feet.
Then stick me in a wombat hole
(an empty one, that's best),
and leave me where the dingos roam
among the scrub out west.

And if youse 'ave a wake fer me
around a blazin' fire
beneath the stars, make sure you do
"Jack Dunn Of Nevertire".
Some Gordon, C.J.Dennis too,
some Banjo and the rest.
Then bid yer ol' mate 'Fond-A-Doo'...
an' let me get some rest!

The Battler

Now the 'little aussie battler' has been praised in song and rhyme,
but a true-blue aussie battler doesn't battle *all* the time.
He's a bloke who proves his mettle when the going's getting tough.
When what's needed is hard yakka, *that's* the time he shows his stuff.

He's the one who's at your shoulder when your back's against the wall.
When the chips are down he stands up, while around him, others fall.
You won't know him by his clothing if you meet him in the street.
He won't always be surrounded by the bush and dust and heat.

No, he comes from town *and* country. His abode's not always fixed.
His religeous views are varied and his ancestry is mixed.
But you'll know him if you need him; if the gods of fate conspire
to bring about misfortune, whether storm or flood or fire.

When the whole world seems against you, and it seems it's got you beat,
he's the first to offer comfort and to help you find your feet.
When you're down to your last dollar, he's the one who helps you out.
He's the first to donate fodder when your stock's been hit by drought.

When the floods are all around you, and you don't know what to do,
it's the battler risks his own life to go in and rescue you.
When you've lost the lot to bushfire, only ashes left instead,
and you're shattered and bewildered, he's the one gives you a bed.

And we couldn't do without them, (half the time this 'he' is a 'she')
If these 'battlers' weren't amongst us, hard to know just where we'd be.
When the 'Reaper' comes to fetch them, and their testament is read:
"Here's a true-blue aussie battler". Nothing else will need be said.

Owed To A Farmer's Wife

It's fifty years that we've been wed;
it's time, I s'pose, some things were said
about the girl who's helped me with the load.
You've been as steady as a rock
with helpin' with the fields and stock,
and so I've gone and written you this ode.....

Oh! Dear to me, my love art thou;
as dear to me as my prize cow.
Yes, dear to me, and precious too,
as my prize pig, my love, are you.

Yes, dear to me, your flowing locks
as any fine merino flocks.
Yes, dear to me, my love is how
you work so well behind the plough.

Yes, dear to me, my love, thou art.
(and handy with a horse and cart.)
Yes dear to me, my love, you've bin....
oops!..time you brought the milkers in.

The Angel Of The Outback

Nancy Bird Walton (b.1915 d.2009)

So Nancy Bird has left us? (Left us poorer I'll be blowed!)
We've lost the greatest aviatrix Australia ever knowed.
The Angel of the Outback's swapped her wings for heaven's kind,
while we assess the legacy that Nancy's left behind.

in '35 she took off...it was Smithy taught her how.
(Australia's greatest hero, they don't make them like him now.)
She rose into our southern skies, on shiny bright new wings.
A queen to share the air's domain, that then was ruled by kings.

At just nineteen she barnstormed in a little Gipsy Moth
made of hickory and leather and a covering of cloth.
Then wheeled her flimsy craft across the Border Country skies.
The Angel of the Outback... Nancy Bird, with laughing eyes.

A landing in a paddock, strewn with rabbit holes unseen...
or 'Back o' Bourke' on claypans where no plane had ever been...
to far-flung picnic races, or a little country show...
if it meant it kept her flying, that's where Nancy Bird would go.

Pioneering the Air Ambulance, pioneering mercy flights.
Pioneering Far West Chidren's Scheme, pioneering equal rights.
An indepenant spirit, and a girl who knew her mind.
A rare 'Bird', and the finest. A true 'one of a kind'.

There's many who will miss her, many more are in her debt.
The virgin fields she furrowed are still bearing their fruit yet.
So Nancy Bird has left us, never more to grace our skies.
The Angel of the Outback... Nancy Bird, with laughing eyes.

..........Happy Landings Nancy.

The Galloping Ghost Of Michael Malone

The galloping ghost of young Michael Malone
rides endlessly over the highlands alone,
to pay for dark deeds and old sins to atone,
by moonlight in high mountain passes.

The story begins, so the local men say,
at Bannister's place on a clear Autumn day.
Rough riders had come there to work for their pay
where steers graze on sweet alpine grasses.

The cattle had spent a long Summer up there,
but now came a chill in the May morning air.
The wind-blasts of Winter would shortly declare
an end to the Autumn's brief glory.

Young Mick, he was green and his horse it was too,
with plenty to prove; that was Old Varney's view.
Said Mick " I'll be there and I'll stick right by you
into and beyond Purgatory."

And so there were ten who rode out that fine day...
with hard work before them to earn their day's pay.
For Bannister said " I'm the one with the say,
and Mick you'll be riding beside 'em ".

Mid-morning they stopped on the mountain's west flank.
A brew and a smoke by a stream's rocky bank.
As each of them sat and as each of them drank,
the tension was building inside 'em.

The party split up into five teams of two,
with one of them being a trusted hand who
had ridden the country before, and who knew
the places the beasts would be grazing.

But changes come quick in the cool mountain air
and stormy black clouds were soon gathering there.
They knew that they didn't have much time to spare,
and so set their stock-whips a'blazing.

"A hundred or so seems to be mighty few.
We haven't much time. It'll just have to do.
If we are not home when this rainstorm comes through,
it's sure that we'll have us a battle."

The thunder-claps rolled and the lightening bolts flashed,
by cold blinding rain, man and beast were now lashed.
To head off stampede, all the riders now dashed
to hold back the terrified cattle.

" Now Mick, we must head them if we are to win;
to earn a man's wages and bring the mob in."
But Mick turned and left them, to save his own skin,
in spite of the fine oath he'd given.

The mob, in the river, in panic wheeled round
and rushed at the riders still holding their ground.
Disaster then struck when a young stockman drowned
when over the bank he was driven.

And while the remainder of Mick's team-mates stood
against the crazed mob and did all that they could
to get back control, though alas never would,
young Mick was bent only on fleeing.

Old Varney, he cursed as he saw Michael run :
" Your soul shall feel torment for what you have done.
May you ride on forever, yet not see the sun."
...the curse welling up from his being.

Distracted and upset by Varney's request,
a feeling of dread and of guilt in his chest,
Mick crashed through some thick scrub that hid the spur's crest
...beyond it a drop-off was waiting.

The galloping ghost of young Michael Malone
still endlessly rides the bare hills to atone
for oaths that were broken while still flesh and bone,
his torment of soul unabating.

La Stupenda

Joan Sutherland b. 1926 d. 2010

We, who watched and listened
from 'the Gods' in raptured bliss
farewell our home-grown goddess
with this reverential kiss,
blown across the footlights
that your luminance outshone...
Dame Joan, our 'La Stupenda'.
We are poorer now you're gone.

.....ooo0ooo.....

Blue Singlet and Stubbies and Socks

You know us as Johnno or Nugget or Norm,
we're seen at the markets or docks.
You'll soon recognise us by our uniform:
blue singlet and stubbies and socks.

We're manual labourers, used to the grind,
we've come through the school of hard knocks.
Where there is hard yakka, it's there that you'll find
blue singlets and stubbies and socks.

You'll see us on building sites shifting the load
of lumber or gravel or rocks;
We're movin' your furniture; fixin' the road
in singlets and stubbies and socks.

Our stubbies are tight..well you know what I mean
us navvies, we're all built like jocks.
Our socks are the colours of our footy team,
don't knock 'em or we'll do our blocks.

We're all built like bulls but we're sly like the fox...
we all swear like troopers with language that shocks...
we do the hard yards while we whistle at frocks...
blue singlets and stubbies and socks!

Kindness and Courage

What is it 'bout Australians when the chips are really down;
when Nature vents her fury on the country or the town;
or liberty is threatened by some mad fanatic mob…
sees us simply gird our loins up as we get on with the job?

These last two years, we've seen it. There's been lots of it about,
as fire and flood and cyclone marked the end to years of drought.
And the scale of these disasters, in their fearsomeness and scope,
tested to its very limits our capacity to cope.

But, in every single instance people right across this land,
without any hesitation, volunteered a helping hand.
Professional and tradesman; rich and poor; the young and old
stepping up to help their neighbour; stretching out a hand to hold.

While the victims in their hardship, more with courage than with pride,
pointed out somebody worse off, putting their own pain aside.
Facing up to their adversity with stoic strength and grace...
the loss of friends and loved ones that no kindness could replace.

Where does this spirit spring from? In what foundry was it made?
The kindness and the courage that so many have displayed?
I think of our bush swagmen. They were icons from a time
when to whinge about your problems seemed to be a sort of crime.

They'd often tramp a hundred miles in hope of getting work
on some isolated station 'on the other side o' Bourke.'
Sheer will and desperation kept them breathing in and out,
when down upon their uppers and their very souls in doubt.

But meet another traveller on the lonesome, weary track,
and they'd share their meagre rations to survive the harsh outback.
Share their campfire and tobacco and their little bit of tea.
Share their yarns and local knowledge...share their sheer humanity.

They say this is the 'Age of Greed'; the selfless breed are gone.
The old aussie swagman spirit, though, in most of us lives on.
There's a well-spring of compassion that lies hidden most the time
beneath the country coat of dust, the city's grit and grime.

It's waiting there, beneath the crust…a strong but dormant seed.
Waiting for its time to sprout; the time of utmost need.
When strangers who have suffered through some cruel twist of fate
become our friends and neighbours, putting "mateship" into "mate".

When Dogs of War snarl at the door, demanding sacrifice…
it's then that spirit rises up to pay the *highest* price.
Adam Lindsay Gordon saw it. He said "Two things stand like stone:
kindness in another's trouble…courage in your own."

By Barrenjoey Light

By Barrenjoey light, my boys, we'll steer our whaler right
and row our contraband ashore in Broken Bay tonight.
The Moon has winked her eye, my boys, and low clouds closin' in
will hide our prize from pryin' eyes...our whisky, rum and gin.

Our whisky, rum and gin, my lads to sell in Sydney Town...
each cask will line our pockets, lads, each puncheon worth a crown.
But if the Customs catch us lads, t'were better that we drown.
Each cask will be a millstone then, with chains to drag us down.

By Barrenjoey Light, my lads,
yer life's not worth a crown
with millstones all around yer necks
with chains to drag yer down.

With chains to drag us down, my boys, our mischief to repay
with labour on the Northern Road for twelve years and a day...
a'breakin' rocks for buildin' blocks to make the Queen's highway.
So cut your water clean, my boys, or give the game away.

You'll give the game away, my lads, a splash will seal our doom.
The good ship Fair Barbadian is fadin' in the gloom.
She's headin' for the open sea...it's time we were away.
Though she'll not keep us company, the Harbourmaster may.

By Barrenjoey Light, my lads,
it's time we were away.
The Harbourmaster guards the door
that leads to Broken Bay.

It's time we were away, my boys, with rowlocks greased and oiled.
And if I hear a grunt or curse, I'll see yer livers broiled.
I'll see yer livers broiled, my boys, and served up on a plate.
So haul away for Broken Bay...the rest is up to fate.

The rest is up to fate, my lads, and wind and wave and rip.
So bend yer backs, and give my lads the Customs Men the slip.
Our cave above the hidden cove will be a welcome sight...
and far behind when morning comes the Barrenjoey Light.

By Barrenjoey Light, my boys,
we steer our course tonight...
and in our wake the Customs Men
and Barrenjoey Light.

Smuggling was a thriving trade during the early years of the young colony of New South Wales. Broken Bay to the north of Sydney offered convenient access by sea, numerous sandy beaches to land the contraband, and a wealth of hiding places among the bush and caves along its shores. At that time there was no lighthouse on Barrenjoey Headland at the entrance to the bay, only a simple red lamplight shown in the window of a cottage at the summit as an aid to navigation. The schooner "Fair Barbadian" was involved in a notorious incident of large scale smuggling of illicit rum and spirits which ultimately led to the establishment of a customs post at the foot of Barrenjoey Headland.

Ballad of the Bikers' Barbecue

Decked out in leather riding gear,
he's a knight of the open road.
He rode one day, so the legends say,
to a meet with a precious load.

Now, the cold wind blows, as the bikie knows,
all things towards the rear.
Any droplets froze on a rider's nose
will wind up in his ear.

Oh, the day was chill, but with iron will
he rode to the bikers' meet.
Where mates he knew, who were riders too,
would be bringing the beer and meat.

Though the road was rough, he was tough enough...
these bikers know no fear.
But the droplets chilled by the chill wind filled
his ear so he could not hear.

He was in a state, for the hour grew late,
so onward his steel steed flew.
For the precious load on the bike he rode
was of eggs for the barbecue.

But he could not hear from his frozen ear
the sound of the cracking eggs
that were meant to be fried at the end of his ride
to go with the steak and kegs.

And the legend tells of the broken shells,
the result of the risk he gambled.
How the bikers met and the eggs that they et
were, sadly, not fried but scrambled.

(a true story)

A Close Call

(Dad's version of events)

When you've married orf five daughters- only one fish left ter fry-
livin' way out in the back-blocks, you don't let a chance go by.
When this young cove comes a'lookin' fer some grub an' 'onest work,
I sees me chance to off-load my last girl on this young turk.

Mum serves 'im up some tucker an' I shows 'im where ter doss.
Tells 'im "See yez at five-thirty". He sez "Righto! Thank yer Boss."
'Round dawn I sends off Charlene, who I've put wise to the plan,
an' she gives a country welcome to the unsuspectin' man.

I only waits five minutes 'fore I bursts into the shed
with me shotgun at the ready an' I hollers..."Dead or Wed?"
Well, the look on this young feller, standin' in 'is birthday suit...
thought e'd die of shock an' 'orror, an' I'd 'ave no need ter shoot.

So I feels a bit remorseful an I lowers down me gun...
but 'e only grabs 'is trousers an' 'e takes orf at the run.
I yells: "Hold fast, ya mongrel, or so 'elp me Gawd, I'll fire!"
But 'e shoots through like a Bondi Tram, 'eadin' for Balranald Shire.

Well, I'm far too old to chase 'im, so I lets me pig-dogs loose.
But the dust that bloke was raisin', I could see it weren't no use.
'E waz 'alf-way back ter Sydney, an' my girl would 'ave ter wait.
So I went an' 'ung the sign up, "Workers Wanted" on the gate.

Four-piece Suits

It's quite clear to all and sundry
that his roots are in the country
when you see him dressed up in his four-piece suits.
Though the city-slickers snigger,
he cuts quite a dashing figure
in his hat and shirt and trousers and elastic-sided boots.

He's a gun-hand, he's a Ringer, he's a gen-u-wine humdinger
in his hat and shirt and trousers and elastic-sided boots.

He don't feel like he's dressed proper
without his Akubra topper...
it's the hat that sets the country lad apart.
It's an oversized felt thimble,
but a true-blue aussie symbol,
and the ladies all agree "Don't he look smart!"

Made of rabbit skin or leather,
handy in all kinds of weather,
it has all the ladies tremblin' at the knees.
And it's handy when he's gotta
use it as a blowfly swatter...
and it keeps his hair from blowin' in the breeze.

You can see the ladies smilin' at his R M Williams stylin'.
In his hat and shirt and trousers and elastic-sided boots.

With his biceps big as boulders,
shirts fit snug across his shoulders
in a pastel, stripe or in a country check.
With two pockets on the breast where
he displays his manly chest-hair,
with at least three buttons undone at the neck.

Pants in denim or in moleskin,
here the *buckle* is the whole thing,
mounted on a handsome, hand-tooled leather belt.
Takes the buckle as his guide ’n
hooks his thumbs in either side ’n
just you watch the ladies’ heart-strings start to melt.

You can hear the ladies chuckle at the size of his belt buckle,
in his hat and shirt and trousers and elastic-sided boots.

Now, if you want to *kill* romancein’
when you’re at the woolshed dancein’,
then, by all means wear them shoes done up with laces.
But that notion he’s a’scotchin’...
’lastic-sideds is his option
when he’s puttin’ flighty fillies through their paces.

When it comes to all things indoors
girls is fussy ’bout their clean floors
but when ’lastic sides are sewn into the upper,
it’s much easier and quicker
to give muddy boots the flicker
if some lady asks him home......to have a cuppa.

On a horse or on a dance-floor, he’s the one the ladies go for.
In his hat and shirt and trousers and elastic-sided boots.

So to end my little story,
there he stands in all his glory
in his four-piece suit, so dashin’ an’ so darin’.
Oh! and one more thing worth notin’,
he says when he needs more coatin’
then a Driza-Bone’s the *only* coat worth wearin’!

So come on all you fellas! Chuck your sneakers and umbrellas,
join the fashion trend of wearing four-piece suits.
It’s your heritage and duty, and you’ll look a bloody beauty!
In your hat and shirt and trousers...and elastic-sided boots.

Finale

So we come to the finale.
It's not Shakespeare *nor* Bob Marley!
I admit there is no "Hanrahan" or "Clancy".
It's the best that I could proffer
and I only hoped to offer
some little rhymes that just might take your fancy.

Thanks for listening...
Will Moody.

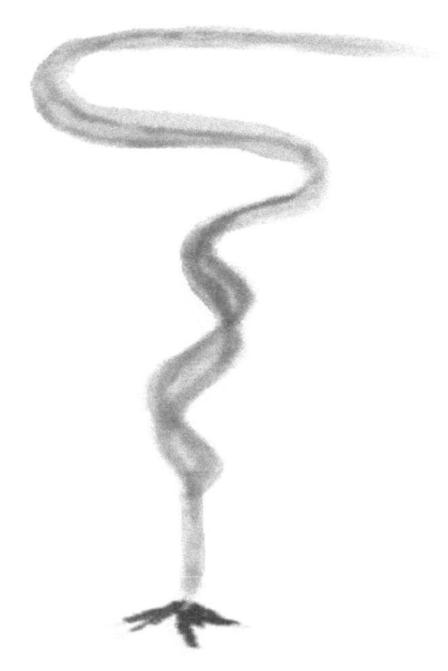

Credits

" The Battler"
selected for inclusion in The Bronzed Swagman Awards Book of Bush Verse 2009

"The Galloping Ghost of Michael Malone"
highly commended, Upper Lachlan Bush Poets Wool Wagon Awards 2009

"A Song That Lingers On"
winner, Henry Lawson Festival Emerging Poet Award 2010

"The Great Australian Hole"
winner, 'Humerous Section' Hunter Bush Poets written competition 2010

"C J Dennis Style"
2nd place, 'Open Section' Toolangi C J Dennis Poetry Festival 2010

"The Regent Bowerbird"
3rd place, 'Birds of the Singing Gardens' Toolangi C J Dennis Poetry Festival 2010

"Cold Campfires"
commended, Eastwood / Hills FAW Boree Log Awards for Bush Verse 2010

"By Barrenjoey Light"
commended, Eastwood / Hills FAW Boree Log Awards for Bush Verse 2010

"Chance or Choice"
commended, Laura Literary Awards 2010

"Have-a-Chat"
highly commended, The Blackened Billy Verse Competition 2010

"Clearance Sale"
highly commended, The Blackened Billy Verse Competition 2011

"Language"
winner, 'Open Section, Poetry ' Bayside Writing Festival 2012

www.ingramcontent.com/pod-product-compliance
Ingram Content Group UK Ltd.
Pitfield, Milton Keynes, MK11 3LW, UK
UKHW020127250726
13967UKWH00002B/511